FLAT STANLEY

Stanley and the Magic Lamp

Stanley and the Magic Lamp

Originally published as *A Lamp for the Lambchops*

Text copyright © 1983 by Jeff Brown
Illustrations by Macky Pamintuan, copyright © 2010 by HarperCollins Publishers
All rights reserved.

Published in agreement with the author, c/o BAROR INTERNATIONAL, INC., Armonk, New York, U.S.A. through Danny Hong Agency, Seoul, Korea.

ISBN 979-11-86701-39-3 14740

Longtail Books

FLAT STANLEY

Stanley and the Magic Lamp

by Jeff Brown
Pictures by Macky Pamintuan

For Elizabeth Tobin
—J.B.

CONTENTS

Prologue

Once upon a very long time ago, way before the beginning of today's sort of people, there was a **magical kingdom** in which everyone lived forever, and anyone of **importance** was a genie,★ mostly the **friendly** kind. The few **wicked** genies kept

---

★**genie** 지니. 아라비아 신화에 나오는 병이나 램프 속에 사는 요정.

out of **sight** in **cave**s or at the **bottom**s of rivers. They had no wish to **provoke** the great Genie King, who **rule**d from a **palace** with many towers and **courtyard**s and gardens with **reflect**ing **pool**s.

The Genie King was **noted** for his **patience** with the **high-spirited** genie princes of the kingdom, but the Genie Queen thought he was much *too* patient with them. She said so one morning in the **throne** room, where the King was studying **report**s and **proposal**s for new magic **spell**s.

"**Discipline**, that's what they need!" She **adjust**ed the Magic Mirror on the throne room wall. "Florts and collibots!* **Grant**ing wishes, which they'll be doing one day, is serious work."

"Florts yourself! You're too **hard on** the
lads," said the King, and then he **frown**ed.
"However, this report here says that one
of them has been behaving very badly
indeed."

"Haraz, right?" said the Queen. "He's a
real **smarty**!"

The Genie King sent a thought to
summon Prince Haraz, which is all such a
ruler has to do when he wants somebody,
and a moment later the young genie flew
into the throne room, did a triple **flip**, and
hovered in the air before the throne.

"What's up?" he asked, **grin**ning.

★ **florts and collibots** 저자가 만든 감탄사. 세상에! 맙소사!

"You are!" said the Queen. "Come down here!"

"No problem," said Haraz, **land**ing.

"It seems you have been playing a great many magical **joke**s," said the King, **tap**ping the reports before him. "Very *annoy*ing jokes, such as causing the army's carpets to fly only in **circle**s, which made all my soldiers **dizzy**."

"That was a good one!" laughed Haraz.

"And turning the **Chief Wizard**'s **wand** into a sausage, while he was **cast**ing a **major** spell? You did that?"

"Ha, ha! You should have seen his face!"

"Stop laughing!" cried the Queen. "This is **shameful**! You should be **severe**ly **punish**ed!"

"He's just a boy, **dear**, only two hundred years old," said the King. "But I'll—"

"Who knows what more he's done?" The Queen turned to the Magic Mirror. "Mirror, what other **dumb** jokes has

Haraz played?"

The Magic Mirror **squirt**ed apple juice
all over her face and the front of her dress.

"Ooooohh!" The Queen **whirl**ed around.
"Florts and collibots! I know who's
responsible for that!"

Prince Haraz tried to look sorry, but it
was too late.

"**That does it**!" said the Genie King.
"Lamp **duty** for you, you **rascal**! One
thousand years of service to a lamp." He
turned to the Queen. "How's that, my
dear?"

"Make it two thousand," said the
Queen, drying her face.

13

Prince Haraz

Almost a year had passed since Stanley Lambchop had **gotten over** being flat, which he had become when his big **bulletin board** had **settle**d on him during the night. It had been a **pleasant**, **restful** time for all the Lambchops, as this **particular** evening was.

Dinner was over. In the living room, Mr.

Lambchop looked up from his newspaper. "How nice this is, my **dear**," he said to Mrs. Lambchop, who was **darn**ing socks. "I am enjoying my paper and your **company**, and our boys are studying in their room."

"Let us hope they are," said Mrs. Lambchop. "So often, George, they find **excuse**s not to work."

Mr. Lambchop **chuckle**d. "They *are* **imaginative**," he said.

In their bedroom, Stanley and his younger brother, Arthur, *were* doing homework. They wore **pajamas**, and over his, Arthur also wore his **Mighty** Man T-shirt, which helped him to **concentrate**.

On the desk between them was what

they supposed to be a tea**pot**—a round, rather **squash**ed-down pot with a **curving spout**, and a **knob** on top for lifting. A **wave** had **roll**ed it up onto the beach that summer, right to Stanley's feet; and since Mrs. Lambchop was very **fond** of old **furniture** and **silverware**, he had saved it as a gift for her birthday, now only a week away.

The pot was painted dark green, but **streak**s of **brownish** metal showed through. To see if **polish**ing would make it shine, Stanley **rub**bed the knob with his pajama **sleeve**.

Puff! Black smoke came from the spout.

"**Yipe**!" said Arthur. "It's going to **explode**!"

"Teapots don't explode." Stanley rubbed again. "I just—"

Puff! Puff! Puff! They came **rapid**ly now, joining to form a small cloud in the air above the desk.

"**Look out**!" Arthur shouted. "Double yipes!"

The black cloud **swirl**ed, its blackness becoming a **mixture** of brown and blue, and began to lose its cloud shape. Arms appeared, and legs, and a head.

"Ready or not, here I come!" said a clear young voice.

Now the cloud was completely gone, and a **slender**, **cheerful**-looking boy **hover**ed in the air above the desk. He wore a sort of **decorate**d towel on his head, a

loose blue shirt, and **curious, flap**ping brown **trousers**, one leg of which had **snag**ged on the pot's spout.

"Florts!" said the boy, shaking his leg. "Collibots! I got the puffs right, and the **scary** cloud, but— There!" Unsnagged, he **float**ed down to the floor and **bow**ed to Stanley and Arthur.

"Who rubbed?" he asked.

Neither of the brothers could speak.

"Well, *someone* did. Genies don't just **drop in**, you know." The boy bowed again. "How do you do? I am Prince Fawzi Mustafa Aslan Mirza Melek Namerd Haraz. Call me Prince Haraz."

Arthur **gasp**ed and **dive**d under his bed.

"What's the matter with him?" the genie asked. "And who are you, and where am I?"

"I'm Stanley Lambchop, and this is the United States of America," Stanley said. "That's Arthur under the bed."

"Not a very **friendly** welcome," said Prince Haraz. "Especially for someone who's been **coop**ed **up** in a lamp." He rubbed the back of his neck. "Florts! One thousand years, with my **knee**s right up against my **chin**. This is my first time out."

"I must have gone crazy," said Arthur from under the bed. "I am just going to lie here until a doctor comes."

"Actually, Prince Haraz, you're here **by accident**," Stanley said. "I didn't even know that pot was a lamp. Was it the rubbing? Those puffs of smoke, I mean, that **turn**ed **into** you?"

"Were you **scare**d?" The genie laughed. "Just a few puffs, I thought, and I'll *whoooosh* up the spout."

"Scaring *me* wasn't fair," said Arthur, staying under the bed. "I just live in this room because Stanley's my brother. It's his lamp, and he's the one who rubbed it."

"Then he's the one I **grant** wishes for," said Prince Haraz. "Too bad for you."

"I don't care," said Arthur, but he did.

"Can I wish for anything?" Stanley asked. "Anything at all?"

"Not if it's **cruel** or evil, or really **nasty**," said Prince Haraz. "I'm a lamp genie, you see, and we're the good kind. Not like those big **jar** genies. They're **stinker**s."

"Wish for something, Stanley." Arthur sounded **suspicious**. "**Test** him **out**."

"I'll be right back," Stanley said, and went into the living room.

"Hey!" he said to Mr. and Mrs. Lambchop. "Guess what?"

"**Hay** is for horses, Stanley, not people," Mr. Lambchop said from behind his newspaper. "Try to remember that."

"Excuse me," Stanley said. "But you'll never guess—"

"My guess is that you and Arthur have not yet finished your homework," said Mrs. Lambchop, looking up from her **mend**ing.

"We were doing it," said Stanley, talking very fast, "but I have this pot that **turn**ed **out** to be a lamp, and when I rubbed it, smoke came out, and then a genie, and he says I can wish for things, only I thought I should ask you first. Arthur got scared, so he's hiding under the bed."

Mr. Lambchop chuckled. "When your

studying is done, my boy," he said. "But no **treasure chest**s full of gold and diamonds, please. Think of the **tax**es we would pay!"

"There is your answer, Stanley," said Mrs. Lambchop. "Now back to work, please."

"Okay, then," said Stanley, going out.

Mrs. Lambchop laughed. "Treasure chests, indeed! Taxes! George, you are very **amusing**."

Behind his newspaper, Mr. Lambchop smiled again. "Thank you, my dear," he said.

The Askit Basket

"I told them, but they didn't believe me," Stanley said, back in the bedroom.

"Of course they didn't." Arthur was still under the bed. "Who'd believe a whole person could **puff** out of a **pot**?"

"It's not a *pot*," said Prince Haraz. "Now please come out. I **apologize** for the puffs."

Arthur **crawl**ed from under the bed.
"No more **scary stuff**?"

"I promise," the genie said, and they shook hands.

Arthur could **hardly** wait now. "Stanley! Try a wish!"

"We can't," Stanley said. "Not till our homework is done."

"What's homework?" asked Prince Haraz.

The brothers **stare**d at him, **amaze**d, and then Stanley explained. The genie shook his head.

"*After* schooltime, when you could be having fun?" he said. "Where I come from, we just let Askit Baskets do the work."

"Well, whatever *they* are, I wish I had

one," said Stanley, forgetting he was not supposed to wish.

Prince Haraz laughed. "Oh? Look behind you."

Turning, Stanley and Arthur saw a large **straw** basket, about the size of a beach ball and **decorate**d with red and green **zigzag stripe**s, **float**ing in the air above the desk.

"**Yipe**s!" said Arthur. "More scary stuff!"

"Don't be **silly**," said the genie. "It's a perfectly **ordinary** Askit Basket. Whatever you want to know, Stanley, just ask it."

Feeling rather **foolish**, Stanley **lean**ed forward and spoke to the basket. "I, uh . . . that is . . . uh . . . Can I have the answers

for my math homework? It's the problems on page twenty of my book."

The basket made a **steady** *huuuummmm* sound, and then a man's voice rose from it, deep and rich like a TV **announcer**'s.

"Thank you for calling Askit Basket," it said. "We're sorry, but all our Answer Genies are busy at this time. Your questions will be answered by the first **available personnel**. While you wait, enjoy a selection by the Genie-ettes.★"

Stanley stared at the Askit Basket. Music was coming out of it now, the sort of soft, **faraway** music he had heard in the

---

★ **Genie-ette** genie에 '작은 것'을 나타내는 접미사 '—ette'를 붙여 작은 요정을 가리키는 말로 쓰였다.

elevators of big office buildings.

Prince Haraz **shrug**ged. "What can you
do? It's a very popular service."

There was a *click* and the music
stopped. Now a female voice, full of
bouncy good **cheer**, came from the basket.
"Hi! This is Shireen! Thanks a whole

bunch for waiting, and I would like at this time to give you your answers. The first answer is: 5 pears, 6 apples, 8 bananas. The second answer is: Tom is 4 years old, Tim is 7, Ted is 11. The third—"

"Wait!" Stanley shouted. "I can't remember all this!"

"A written record, created especially for your **convenience**, is in the basket, sir," said the **cheery** voice. "Thanks for calling Askit Basket, and have a real nice day!"

Lifting the **lid** of the basket, Stanley saw a **sheet** of paper with all his answers on it. "Oh, good!" he said. "Thank you. Can my brother talk now, please?"

Arthur **clear**ed **his throat**. "Hello, Shireen," he said. "This is Arthur Lambchop speaking. For English, I'm supposed to write about 'What I Want to Be.'"

"Certainly, Mr. Lambchop," said the basket. "Just a **teeny** moment now, to make sure the **handwriting**—There! All done!"

Arthur opened the basket and found a

sheet of **lined** paper **cover**ed with his own handwriting. He read it aloud.

What I Want to Be
by Arthur Lambchop

When I grow up, I want to be **President** of the United States so that I can make a law not to have any more wars. And get to meet **astronaut**s. And I would like not to have to go out with girls who want to get all **dressed up**. Most of all I would like to be the strongest man in the world, like **Mighty** Man, not to hurt people, but so everybody would be **extra** nice to me.

The End

Arthur smiled. "That's fine!" he said. "Just what I wanted to say, Shireen."

"Good," said the basket. "'Bye now! Have a super day!"

The brothers called good-bye, and Prince Haraz **pluck**ed the basket out of the air and set it on the desk by his lamp.

"There! Homework's done," he said. "That was a very ordinary sort of wish, Stanley. Isn't there anything special you've always wanted? Something exciting?"

Stanley knew right away what he wanted most. He had always loved animals; how exciting it would be to have his own zoo! But that would **take up** too much space, he thought. Just one animal then, a truly unusual **pet**. A lion? Yes!

What fun it would be to walk down the street with a pet lion on a **leash**!

"I wish for a lion!" he said. "Real, but **friendly**."

"Real, but friendly," said the genie. "No problem."

Stanley **realize**d suddenly that a lion would **scare** people, and that an elephant would be even greater fun.

"An elephant, I mean!" he shouted. "Not a lion. An elephant!"

"What?" said Prince Haraz. "An eleph—? Oh, collibots! Look what you made me do!"

A most unusual head had formed in the air across the room, a head with an elephant's **trunk** for a nose but with small,

neat, lionlike ears. There was a lion's **mane** behind the head, but then came an elephant's body and legs in a **brownish**-gold lion color, and finally a little gray elephant **tail** with a pretty gold **ruff** at the **tip**. All together, these parts made an animal about the size of a medium lion or a small elephant.

"My **goodness**!" said Stanley. "What's that?"

"A Liophant." Prince Haraz seemed **annoy**ed. "It's your fault, not mine. You **overlap**ped your wish."

The Liophant opened his mouth wide, gave a half **roar**, half **snort** *Grrowll-HONK!* that made them all jump, then sat back on his **hind** legs and went *pant-pant* like a puppy, looking quite nice.

"Well, we got the friendly part right," said the genie. "The young ones mostly are."

Stanley **pat**ted him, and Arthur **tickle**d behind the neat little ears. The Liophant **lick**ed their hands and Stanley was not at all sorry that he had **mix**ed **up** his wish.

Just then, a **knock** sounded on the

bedroom door, and Mrs. Lambchop's voice called out, "Homework done?"

"Come in," said Stanley, not thinking, and the door opened.

"How very quiet you—" Mrs. Lambchop began, and then she stopped. Her eyes moved slowly about the room from Prince Haraz to the Askit Basket, and on to the Liophant.

"**Gracious**!" she said.

Prince Haraz made a little **bow**. "How do you do? You are the mother of these fine **lad**s, yes?"

"I am, thank you," said Mrs. Lambchop. "Have we met? I don't seem to—"

"This is Prince Haraz," Stanley said. "And that's a Liophant, and that's an Askit

Basket."

"Guess what," said Arthur. "Prince Haraz is a genie, and Stanley can wish for anything he wants."

"How very **generous**!" Mrs. Lambchop said. "But I'm not sure . . ." Turning, she called into the living room. "George come here! Something quite un**expect**ed has happened."

"In a moment," Mr. Lambchop called back. "I am reading an unusual story in my newspaper, about a duck who watches TV."

"This is even more unusual than that," she said, and Mr. Lambchop came **at once**.

"Ah, yes," he said, looking about the room. "Yes, I see. Would someone care to explain?"

"I tried to before," Stanley said. "Remember? About—"

"Wait, **dear**," said Mrs. Lambchop.

The Liophant had been making **snuffling**, hungry sounds, so she went off to the kitchen and returned with a large **bowl** full of hamburger mixed with warm milk. While the Liophant ate, Stanley told Mrs. Lambchop what had happened.

Mr. Lambchop thought for a moment. "Unusual indeed," he said. "And what a fine opportunity for you, Stanley. But I do not **approve** of using the Askit Basket for your homework, boys. Nor will your teachers, I'm afraid."

"My plan is, let's not tell them," Arthur

said.

Mr. Lambchop gave him a long look. "Would you take **credit** for work you have not done?"

Arthur **blush**ed. "Oh! Well, I guess not . . . I wasn't thinking. Because of all the excitement, you know?"

Mr. Lambchop wrote NOT IN USE on a piece of **cardboard** and **tape**d it to the Askit Basket.

"It is too late for more wishing tonight," Mrs. Lambchop said. "Prince Haraz, there is a **fold**ing **cot** in the **closet**, so you will be comfortable here. Tomorrow is Saturday, which we always spend together in the park. You will join us, yes?"

"Thank you very much," said the genie,

and he helped Stanley and Arthur **set up** the cot.

The Liophant was already asleep, and Mrs. Lambchop picked up his bowl. "Gracious! Three pounds★ of the best hamburger, and he ate every bit." She **put out** the light. "Good night to you all."

It was quite dark in the bedroom, but some moonlight shone through the window. From their beds, Stanley and Arthur could see that Prince Haraz was still sitting up in his cot. For a moment all was silence **except** for the gentle **snoring** of the Liophant, and then the genie said, "Sorry about the snoring. It's having all

★ **pound** 무게의 단위 파운드. 1파운드는 약 0.454킬로그램이다.

that nose, probably."

"It's okay," Arthur said sleepily. "Do genies snore?"

"We don't even sleep," said Prince Haraz. "Your mother was so kind, I didn't want to tell her. She might have felt bad."

"I'll try to stay awake, if you want to talk," Stanley said.

"No thanks," said the genie. "I'll be fine. After all those years alone in the lamp, it's nice just having **company**."

In the Park

Everyone slept late and enjoyed a large breakfast, **particular**ly the Liophant, who ate two more pounds of hamburger, five bananas, and three **loaves** of bread.

Then, since all the Lambchops enjoyed tennis, they **set out** with their **racket**s for the **court**s in the big park close by. **Aware** that his genie clothes would **puzzle**

people, Prince Haraz borrowed **slacks** and a shirt from Stanley, and came along.

In the street, they met Ralph Jones, an old **college** friend of Mr. Lambchop's, whom they had not seen for quite some time.

"Nice **run**ning **into** you, George, and you too, Mrs. Lambchop," said Mr. Jones. "Hello, Arthur. Hello, Stanley. Aren't you the one who was flat? **Round**ed out nicely, I see."

"You always did have a fine memory, Ralph," Mr. Lambchop said. "Let me introduce our houseguest, Prince Haraz. He is a **foreign** student, here to study our ways."

"How do you do?" said the genie. "I am Fawzi Mustafa Aslan Mirza Melek

Namerd Haraz."

"How do you do?" Mr. Jones said.
"Well, I must be off. Good-bye, Lambchops.
Nice to have met you, Prince Fawzi Mustafa
Aslan Mirza Melek Namerd Haraz."

"He *does* have a wonderful memory,"
Mrs. Lambchop said as Mr. Jones walked
away.

They set out for the park again.

"How it would surprise Mr. Jones to
learn that Prince Haraz is a genie," Mrs.
Lambchop **remark**ed. "The whole world
would be **amaze**d. **Gracious**! We'd all be
famous, I'm sure."

"I was famous once, when I was flat,"
Stanley said. "I didn't like it after a while."

"I remember," said Mrs. Lambchop.

"**Nevertheless**, I wish I knew myself what being famous feels like."

Prince Haraz looked at Stanley in a **questioning** way, and Stanley gave a little **nod**. The genie smiled and nodded back.

They were just passing the Famous Museum of Art, one of the city's most important buildings. A tour bus, filled with visitors from foreign countries, had stopped before the museum, and a guide was **lecturing** the **passenger**s through a **megaphone**.

"Over where those trees are, that's our great City Park!" he **announce**d. "Here, on the right, is the Famous Museum of Art, full of great paintings and **statue**s and— Oh, what a surprise! We're in luck today,

folks! That's Mrs. George Lambchop, coming right toward us! Harriet Lambchop herself, **in person**! Right there, with the tennis racket!"

The tourists cried out in **pleased astonish**ment, turning in their seats to **stare** where the guide was pointing.

"What—? He means *you*, Harriet!" said Mr. Lambchop.

"I think so," said Mrs. Lambchop. "Oh, my **goodness**! They're coming!"

The tourists were **rush**ing from the bus. A Japanese family **reach**ed Mrs. Lambchop first, all with cameras.

"Please, Lampchop lady," said the husband, **bow**ing **polite**ly. "**Honor** to take picture, yes?"

"Of course," said Mrs. Lambchop. "I hope you are enjoying our country. But why *my* picture? I'm not—"

"No, no! Famous, famous! Famous Lambchop lady!" cried the Japanese family, taking pictures as fast as they could.

Mrs. Lambchop understood suddenly that her wish had been **grant**ed. "Thank you, Prince Haraz!" she said. "What fun!"

She **pose**d graciously for all the tourists and **sign**ed **dozen**s of **autograph**s. In the park she was **recognize**d again, and had to do more posing and signing.

It was now midmorning, and all the park's tennis courts were **occupied**, but the Lambchops' **disappoint**ment **lessen**ed

when they saw a **crowd gather**ed by one court and learned that Tom McRude, the world's best tennis player, was about to lecture and **demonstrate** his **stroke**s. Tom McRude **was known for** his **terrible temper** and bad manners, but the Lambchops were eager to see him nevertheless. With Prince Haraz, they **squeeze**d close to the court, next to the TV-news cameras **cover**ing the event.

"None of you can ever be a great tennis player like me," Tom McRude was saying. "But at least you can have the **thrill** of seeing me."

A little old lady in the crowd gave a **tiny sneeze**, and he **glare**d at her. "What's the matter with you, **granny**?"

The old lady **burst** into tears, and
friends led her away.

"What a **mean fellow**!" Prince Haraz
whispered to Stanley.

"I can't **stand** old sneezing people!" said
Tom McRude. "Okay, now I'll show how I
hit my great forehand!★ First—"

"**Hold it**, Tom!" called the TV-news
director. "We've just **spot**ted Harriet
Lambchop here. What a **break**! Maybe
she'll say a few words for our cameras!"

Even Tom McRude was **impress**ed. "*The*
Harriet Lambchop? Wow!"

"**Swing** those cameras this way,
fellows!" The director ran over to Mrs.

★ forehand 포핸드. 테니스에서 라켓을 쥔 팔 방향으로 오는 공을 받아 치
는 것.

Lambchop, holding out a microphone.

"Wonderful to see you!" he said. "Everybody wants to know your views. Favorite color? What about the foreign situation? Do you sleep in **pajamas** or a nightgown?★"

"Isn't that rather **personal**?" asked Mr. Lambchop.

"George, please. . . ." Mrs. Lambchop spoke into the microphone. "Thank you all for your kind welcome," she said. "I would just like to say that I'm glad my fans are having such a lovely day in this **delightful** park."

The crowd **cheer**ed and **wave**d, and

★ nightgown 여자들이 입는 긴 원피스형 잠옷.

Mrs. Lambchop waved back and **blew kiss**es. **Jealous** of the **attention** she was getting, Tom McRude **whack**ed a tennis ball over the **fence** behind him.

Noticing, Mrs. Lambchop spoke again into the microphone. "And now, let us give this great **champion** our attention!"

"Yeah!" **growl**ed Tom McRude. When the TV cameras had swung back to him, he **went on**. "I need a **volunteer**, so that I can demonstrate how terrible most players are **compare**d to me!"

Mr. Lambchop thought it would be thrilling to share a court with a champion. **Signal**ing with his racket, he stepped forward.

Tom McRude handed him some balls.

"Okay, try a **serve**."

Mr. Lambchop prepared to serve.

"He's got his feet wrong!" Tom McRude shouted. "And his **grip** is wrong! Everything is wrong!"

This made Mr. Lambchop so nervous that he served two balls into the **net** instead of over it.

"Terrible! Terrible! Watch how I do it," said Tom McRude, running to the far side of the court. From there he served five balls, so hard and fast that Mr. Lambchop missed the first four **entire**ly. The fifth one **knock**ed the racket out of his hand.

"Ha, ha!" laughed Tom McRude. "Now let's see you run!"

He began hitting **whiz**zing forehands

and backhands★ at sharp **angle**s across the court, making Mr. Lambchop look **foolish** as he **race**d **back and forth**, getting very red in the face and missing **practical**ly every **shot**.

The other Lambchops grew angry, as did Prince Haraz. "This need not continue, you know," he whispered to Stanley.

Just then, Mr. Lambchop came **skid**ding to a **halt** before them, **bang**ing his **knee** with his racket as he missed yet another of the champion's powerful shots.

"Ha, ha! This is how _I_ give lessons!" shouted Tom McRude.

Mr. Lambchop looked at Stanley, then

★ backhand 백핸드. 탁구나 테니스에서 공을 치는 손의 손등이 상대편을 향하도록 하는 타구법.

at Prince Haraz. "Okay," Stanley said, and the genie smiled a little smile.

"Thank you," said Mr. Lambchop. Returning to the court, he called out to the crowd. "Ladies and gentlemen, I will try my serve again!"

Across the net, Tom McRude gave a **nasty** laugh and **slash**ed his big racket through the air.

Mr. Lambchop served a ball, not into the net this time, but fast as a **bullet** right where it was supposed to go. Tom McRude's mouth fell open as the ball whizzed past him. "Out!" he shouted. "That ball was out!"

Voices rose from the crowd. "**Shame** on you!" . . . "The ball was *in!*" . . . "What a liar!" . . . "In, in, in!"

Tom McRude shook his **fist**. "I'll **bet** you can't do that again!"

Mr. Lambchop served three more balls, each even faster than the first one, and as perfectly placed. Tom McRude could not even touch them, though the last one **bounce**d up into his nose.

Then Mr. Lambchop **rallied** with him, **gliding swift**ly about the court and returning every shot with ease. With powerful forehands, he made Tom McRude run from corner to corner; with little drop shots,★ he drew the champion up to the net, then **lob**bed＊ high shots

---

★ **drop shot** 드롭 샷. 테니스에서 공을 네트 바로 너머로 떨어뜨리는 타법.
＊ **lob** 로브. 테니스에서, 공을 높이 쳐서 상대편의 머리 위로 넘겨 코트의 후방으로 떨어뜨리는 타법.

to send him racing back again. Nobody
has ever played such great tennis as Mr.
Lambchop played that day.

Tom McRude was soon too tired, and
too angry, to continue. He threw down his
racket and jumped on it.

"You're just lucky!" he **yell**ed. "**Besides**,
I have a cold! And the sun was in my eyes
the whole time!" Pushing his way through
the crowd, he ran out of the park.

There was **tremendous** cheering for
Mr. Lambchop, who just smiled **modest**ly
and waved his racket in a **friendly** way.
Then he came over to where the other
Lambchops and Prince Haraz were
standing with the TV-news director.

"You're really *good*," the director said.

"**Frankly**, you looked terrible when you first went out there."

"It takes me a while to get **warm**ed **up**," Mr. Lambchop said, and led his family away.

Leaving the park, Mrs. Lambchop signed many more autographs, and a **reporter** from *Famous Faces* magazine was waiting to interview her at home.

"You'll be on the cover of our next issue," said the reporter. "How much do you **weigh**? Will there be a movie about your life? Who gave you your first kiss?"

"**None of your business**!" said Mr. Lambchop, and the reporter went away.

They watched the evening news on television, hoping Mr. Lambchop's tennis would be shown, but only Mrs. Lambchop appeared, with Tom McRude in the background. "The **celebrated** Harriet Lambchop was in the park today," said the **newscaster**, after which came a **close-up** of Mrs. Lambchop saying, "I'm glad my fans are having such a lovely day," and that was that.

Dinner was **interrupt**ed several times by phone calls for Mrs. Lambchop from newspaper and television people. The calls **bother**ed Mr. Lambchop, but not the Liophant, who ate four pork chops,★ a **jar** of peanut butter, a quart* of potato salad, and the **rubber** mat from under his dish.

★ **pork chop** 돼지 갈비살.
✻ **quart** 부피의 단위 쿼트. 1쿼트는 1갤런의 1/4, 파인트의 2배로 약 0.95리터에 해당한다.

The Brothers Fly

"I'm not **complain**ing," said Arthur, complaining, "but it's not fair. Some people have Liophants, or get famous. I want to be **President**, or as strong as **Mighty** Man, but all I got was one minute with an Askit Basket we can't even use anymore."

It was after dinner, and the brothers were in their bedroom with Prince Haraz,

all in **pajamas**.

"It's not my fault, Arthur." The genie looked hurt. "I just follow orders. **Rub**, I appear. Wish, I **grant**. That's it."

Stanley felt sorry for his brother. "I don't think you should be President, Arthur," he said. "But I'll wish for you to be the strongest man in the world. I wish it, Prince Haraz!"

"Oh, good!" said Arthur.

He waited, but nothing happened. "Darn!★ It didn't work!" **Disappoint**ed, he **punch**ed his left hand with his right **fist**.

"Owwww!" Jumping up and down, Arthur **flap**ped his hand to **relieve** the

---

★ **darn** 'damn(빌어먹을)'을 순화한 단어로, 못마땅하거나 짜증스러울 때 쓰는 표현.

pain.

"When you're the strongest man in the world," said Prince Haraz, "you have to be careful what you hit."

"But I still feel like me," Arthur said. Testing himself, he took hold of the big desk with one hand and lifted it easily above his head.

Stanley's mouth flew open, and so did the desk **drawer**s.

Pencils, **marble**s, and paper **clip**s rained down onto the floor.

"Ooops!" said Arthur.

"This is **ridiculous**," said Prince Haraz, helping him **tidy** up. "The strongest man in the world, in a bedroom picking up desks! Out having **adventure**s, that's where you

should be."

"We can't now," Arthur said. "It's almost **bedtime**."

Stanley had an idea. "There'd be time if we could fly! Can't we all fly somewhere?"

"I've always been able to," said the genie. "For you two, it'll take wishing."

"I wish!" shouted Stanley. "Flying! Arthur and me both!"

For a moment the brothers **held their breath**, **expect**ing to be **swept** up into the air. Then Arthur tried small flapping movements with his **elbow**s.

"Oh, collibots!" said the genie. "Not like that. Just *think* of flying, and where you want to go."

It worked.

Stanley and Arthur found themselves suddenly a few feet★ off the floor, face down and quite comfortable, and however they wished to go, up or down, forward or back, was how they went. It was like swimming in soft, in**visible** water, but without the effort of swimming. Prince Haraz gave advice as the brothers **glide**d happily about the room: "Point your **toe**s. . . . **Heads up**! . . . Good, very good. . . . Yes, I think you're ready now!"

He opened a window and **lean**ed out. "Hmmm. . . . This **breeze** may be coolish higher up. We'd better wear something **extra**."

★ feet 길이의 단위 피트. 1피트는 약 30.48센티미터이다.

Stanley and Arthur put on bath**robe**s and **glove**s, and the genie chose a red parka★ and a dragon-face ski mask. Then he said, "Away we go!" and the brothers **float**ed through the window after him, out into the night.

Up! Up! UP! they went, **level**ing **off** now and then to practice **speed**ing, but mostly rising **steadily** higher. Stanley and Arthur flew **side by side**, **gain**ing **confidence** from each other, and the genie **kept an eye on** them from behind.

It was a beautiful night. The sky above them was full of stars. Below them the lights of the city **twinkle**d as brightly as

★ **parka** 파카. 모자가 달린 짧은 외투.

the stars. The brothers' white bathrobes and the genie's red parka shone in the moonlight.

They flew above the big park, where an **orchestra** was giving a concert. Music floated up to them: the clear, sweet **tone**s of flutes★ and violins and trumpets;✶ the deep, strong **note**s of cymbals✳ and drums.

"Oh, I'm enjoying this!" Prince Haraz called through his dragon mask. "So different from inside that lamp!"

The three fliers **join**ed **hands** and **circle**d the **blaze** of light from where the orchestra sat. It was like ice-skating to

---

★ flute 플루트. 옆으로 쥐고 구멍에 입김을 불어 넣어 소리를 내는 관악기.
✶ trumpet 트럼펫. 직경이 작은 원통형의 관으로 된 금관 악기.
✳ cymbals 심벌즈. 두 개의 원반을 서로 맞부딪혀 소리를 내는 금속 타악기.

music at a **rink**, but much more fun.

In the **distance**, the wing lights of a big airplane **blink**ed across the sky.

"Let's **chase** it!" Stanley shouted.

Prince Haraz laughed. "Go on! I'll **catch up**!"

Whoooosh! Whoooosh! Holding their arms by their sides, Stanley and Arthur **flash**ed like rockets across the sky, their bathrobes flapping like the **sail**s of a boat. The big airplane was fast, but the brothers were faster. Catching up, they flew around and around it, looking through the windows at the **passenger**s reading and eating from **tiny tray**s.

Arthur saw a little girl with a **comic** book. **Zoom**ing close to her window, he

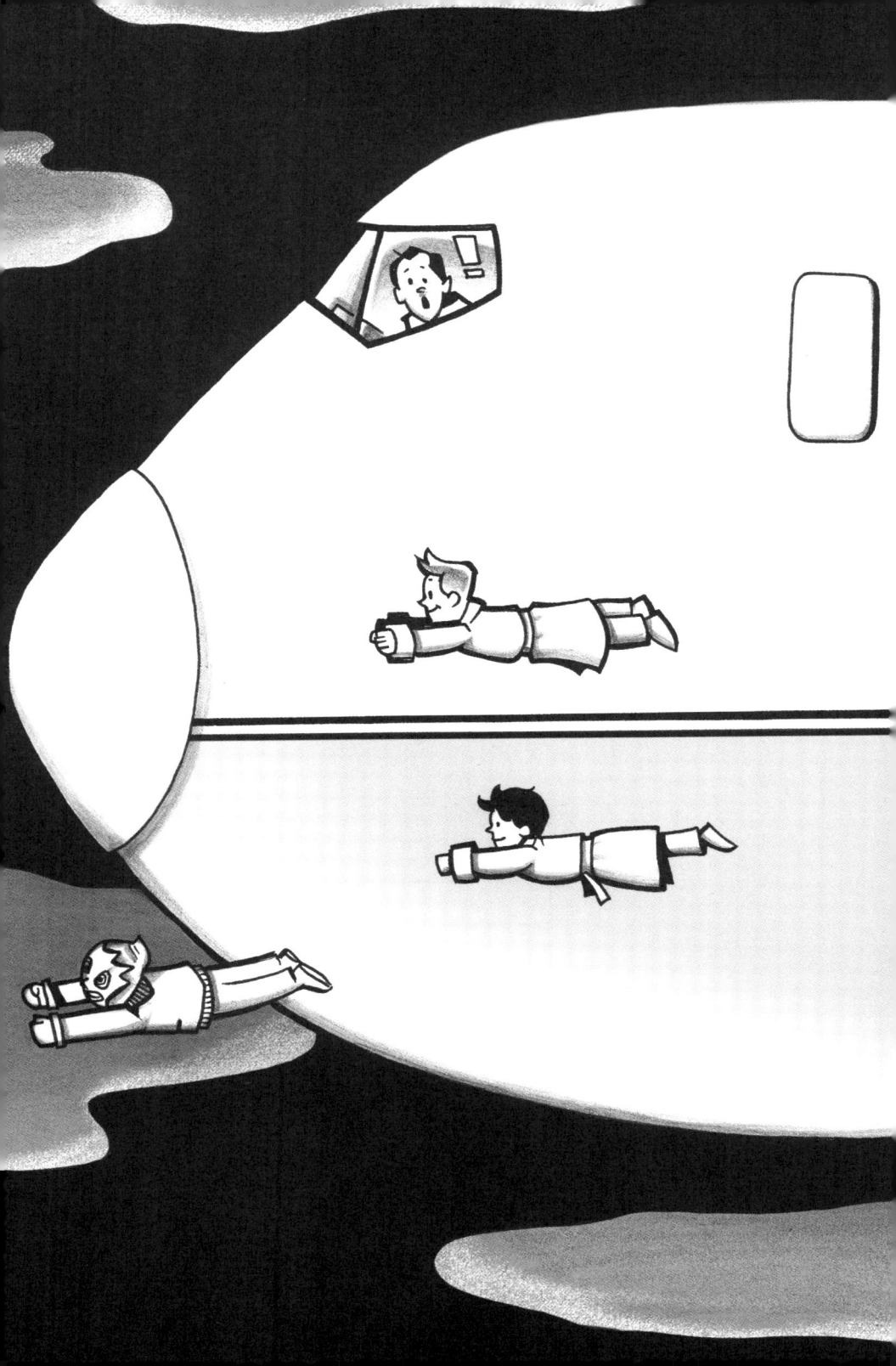

stretched his neck, trying to read over her shoulder. The little girl looked up and saw him. Being **mean**, she held the comic book down where he couldn't see it, and **stuck out** her **tongue**. Arthur stuck his tongue out at her, and the little girl **scowl**ed and pulled a curtain across her window.

On the other side of the plane, Stanley saw a very tired-looking young couple with a crying baby across their **lap**s, keeping them awake. Flying up next to the window so that the baby could see him, he made a funny face, **puff**ing his lips and **wrinkling** his nose. The baby smiled, and Stanley put his **thumb**s in his ears and **wriggle**d his other fingers. The baby smiled again, and went to sleep.

Stanley flew back around the plane, past the **cockpit**, to join Arthur on the other side.

There were two **pilot**s in the cockpit, and one saw Stanley fly by. Turning his head, he now saw both brothers **hover**ing above a wing **tip**, waiting for Prince Haraz to catch up.

"Guess what I see out there, Bert," he said.

"The stars in the sky, Tom, and below us the mighty ocean," replied the other pilot.

"No," said Tom. "Two kids in bathrobes."

"Ha, ha! What a **joke**r!" said Bert, but he turned to look.

Only Prince Haraz could be seen now above the wing, his parka flapping as he looked around for Stanley and Arthur, who were hiding from him behind the plane.

"So what do you see, Bert?" asked Tom, keeping his own eyes straight ahead. "Two kids in bathrobes, right?"

"Wrong," said Bert quietly. "I see a guy in ski clothes, with a dragon face."

The pilots **stare**d at each other, then out at the wing again, but the genie had flown to join the brothers behind the plane.

"Nobody there," said Tom. "Let's never **mention** this to anyone, Bert. Okay?"

"Good idea," said Bert. "**Definite**ly."

They flew on and had nothing more to say.

A giant ocean liner,★ **ablaze** with lights, **made its way** across the sea below.

"Come on!" Arthur shouted, **whiz**zing away with Stanley behind him. Again, Prince Haraz laughed and let them go.

The beauty of the great ship made the brothers **marvel** as they drew near. It was like an **enormous** birthday cake, each **deck** a **layer sparkling** with the brightness of a thousand candles.

"Look, Stanley!" Arthur cried. "They're having a party on the main deck!"

They flew closer to enjoy the fun and saw then that it was not a party, but a **rob**bery.

The main deck was **crowd**ed because

★ **ocean liner** 원양 정기선. 일정한 항로를 정기적으로 운항하는 배.

robbers had **line**d **up** all the passengers and were taking their money and **jewelry**. The helicopter in which the robbers had arrived was parked close by, below the **captain**'s **bridge**. The captain and his **fellow officer**s had **struggle**d, but they were **chain**ed up now on the bridge.

"We've got to do something, Stanley!" Arthur said.

Zooming down to the bridge, he shouted over the **railing** at the robbers below. "Stop, you **crook**s! Give back all that money and jewelry and **stuff**!"

Using his great **strength**, Arthur **tore** away the ropes and chains that **bound** the ship's officers. It was as if he were just tearing paper.

Amazed, the robbers stumbled backward, dropping money and jewelry all over the deck.

"Oh, lordy!" one robber yelled. "Who are you?"

Remembering his favorite comic book hero, Arthur could not resist showing off. He flew ten feet up in the air and stayed there, looking fierce.

"I am Mighty Arthur!" he shouted in a deep voice. "Mighty Arthur, Enemy of Crime!"

Exclamations rose from the robbers and passengers and ship's officers. "So strong, and a flyer too! . . . Who expected Mighty Arthur? . . . Are we ever *lucky!* . . . This ought to be on TV!"

Now Stanley **swoop**ed down from the
sky with his bathrobe belt un**tie**d, so that
his robe **flare**d behind him like a **cape**.
"I'm Mighty Stanley!" he called. "**Defend**er
of the **Innocent**!"

"I do that too!" Arthur cried, wishing
he had made *his* robe a cape. "We both do
good things, but I'm the really strong one!"

He saw suddenly that several robbers were trying to escape in the helicopter. It was already rising, but Arthur flashed through the air until he was directly above it, and with one hand pushed it back down onto the deck. When the **frighten**ed robbers jumped out, the ship's officers **grab**bed them and tied them up.

Now the passengers were even more amazed. "Did you see that?" they said, and "Mighty Arthur and Mighty Stanley, both on the same day!" and "This is *better* than TV!"

The brothers flew up to join Prince Haraz, who had been circling over the ship. "What a pair of show-offs!" said the genie. "Even worse than I used to be."

As they **set out** for home, the **cheer**s of the **grateful** passengers and **crew** floated up behind them. "**Hooray** for our **rescue**rs!" they heard, and "Especially Mighty Arthur!" and a moment later, "Mighty Stanley too, of course!"

Soon the big ship was no more than an **outline** of tiny lights in the black sea below, and the last cheer was only a **whisper** above the **rush**ing of the wind: "Three cheers . . . for . . . the Enemy . . . of . . . Crime . . . and the . . . Defender . . . of the . . . Inno . . . cent!"

The brothers felt very proud, but it had been a **tiring** adventure, and they were not sorry when the city came into **sight**.

The Last Wish

Flying back into the bedroom, the three **adventure**rs found Mr. and Mrs. Lambchop waiting **anxious**ly. The Liophant, who had just finished an **enormous bowl** of spaghetti mixed with chocolate cookies and milk, was asleep.

"**Thank goodness**!" Mrs. Lambchop ran to hug her sons.

"Where have you been?" Mr. Lambchop was **stern**. "Is that you, Prince Haraz, behind that dragon face?"

The genie took off his mask. "Were you worried? Sorry. We went for a little flight."

"Wait till you hear!" said Arthur. "You can't tell from looking, but I'm the strongest man in the world, and—"

"Take off those **robe**s and **glove**s," said Mrs. Lambchop. "It is not wise to get **overheated**."

She **went on**, as they put their things away. "*Such* an evening! The phone never stopped. I was asked to go on four TV shows, and to advertise a new soap—they wanted to photograph me in the bath**tub**, so of course I said no!—and then, to find the window open and the three of you *gone!* Such a **fright**!"

"We thought we'd be right back," said Stanley, **apologizing**. "We didn't know so many exciting things would happen."

Everybody sat down, and Stanley told about wishing Arthur strong, and the flying, and **chasing** the airplane, and the **rob**bers on the ship. Mr. and Mrs. Lambchop both gave deep **sigh**s when Stanley was done.

"It seems, Prince Haraz," Mr. Lambchop said, "that there are often un**expect**ed **consequence**s when wishes come true."

"Oh, yes," said the genie. "That's what got me into a lamp."

"It's not just the Askit Basket problem,"

Mr. Lambchop said. "Mrs. Lambchop has been famous less than a day, and already she is **exhaust**ed and has lost all her **privacy**. And though Tom McRude **deserve**d what he got, his tennis comes from natural ability. I am not proud of having **shame**d him by using magic."

"And Arthur's great **strength** will make other boys afraid of him," Mrs. Lambchop said. "And flying, mixing with **criminal**s . . . **Dear** me! We must consider all this. I will make hot chocolate. It is helpful when there is serious thinking to be done."

Everyone enjoyed the delicious hot chocolate she brought from the kitchen, with a marshmallow* for each cup. The Lambchops sat quietly, **sip**ping and

thinking. Prince Haraz, having said twice that he was sorry to have caused problems, began to **pace** up and down. The Liophant was still asleep.

At last Mr. Lambchop put down his cup and **clear**ed **his throat**. "Your **attention**, please," he said, and they all looked at him.

"Here is my opinion," he said. "Genies and their magic, Prince Haraz, are fine for **faraway** lands and long-ago times, but the Lambchops have always been quite natural people, and this is the United States of America, and the time is today. We are **grateful** for the excitement you

---

★ marshmallow 마시멜로. 젤라틴과 달걀 흰자, 설탕, 향료 등을 섞어 만든 과자. 코코아에 넣어 먹는 경우가 많다.

have offered, but now I must ask: Is it possible for Stanley to *un*wish all the wishes he has made?"

"It is, actually," said the genie.

"How **clever** of you, George!" cried Mrs. Lambchop.

Arthur sighed. "I don't know. . . . I really like the flying. But being so strong, I guess nobody *would* play with me."

"I care most about the Liophant," Stanley said. "Couldn't we just keep him?"

"He is very **lovable**," said Mrs. Lambchop. "But he never stops eating! We cannot *afford* to keep him."

"Sad, but true," Mr. Lambchop said. "Now please tell us, Prince Haraz, what must be done."

"It's called **Reverse** Wishing." The genie took the little green lamp from the desk and turned it over. "The **instruct**ions should be right here on the **bottom**. Let's see. . . ."

He studied the words **carve**d into the bottom of the lamp. "Seems simple enough. Each wish has to be separately reversed. I just say 'Mandrono!' and—" His voice rose. "Oh, collibots! Double florts! See that little circle there? This is a *training* lamp! There may not be enough wishes left!"

"A training lamp?" **exclaim**ed Mr. Lambchop. "What is that?"

"They're for beginners like me, so we don't **overdo** for one person," Prince

Haraz said unhappily. "The little 'fifteen' in the circle, that's all the wishes I'm allowed for Stanley."

The Lambchops all spoke **at once**. "What? . . . You never told us! . . . Only fifteen? . . . Oh, dear!"

"Please, I'm **embarrass**ed enough," said the genie, very red in the face. "A *training* lamp! As if I were a baby!"

"We are all beginners, **at one time or another**," said Mr. Lambchop. "What matters is, are fifteen wishes enough?"

The genie **count**ed on his fingers to be sure he got it right. "Askit Basket, Liophant—lucky he doesn't count double!—that's two, and **fame** for Mrs. Lambchop and the **fancy** tennis, that's four. Making Arthur strong is five, flying for him *and* Stanley is two more . . ." He smiled. "Seven, and seven for reversing is fourteen! One wish **left over** for some sort of good-bye **treat**!"

"Thank goodness!" Mrs. Lambchop **hesitate**d. "It is very late. Could you begin the reversing *now*, do you think?"

Prince Haraz **nod**ded. "I'll do the whole family in a **bunch**. Let's see . . . Strength, famous, tennis, two flying. Ready, Arthur? No more **Mighty** Man after this, I'm afraid."

"Will I feel weak?" Arthur asked. "Will I **flop** over?"

The genie shook his head. "Mandrono!" he said. "Mandrono, Mandrono,

Mandrono, Mandrono!"

Arthur felt a **prickling** on the back of his neck. When the prickling stopped, he gave the big desk a **shove**, but couldn't **budge** it.

"I'm just **regular** me again," he said. "Oh, well."

"And I am just Harriet Lambchop again," said Mrs. Lambchop, smiling. "An unimportant person."

"To all of us, my dear, you are the most important person we know," said Mr. Lambchop. "Arthur, you are as strong as you were yesterday. Think of it that way."

The genie sipped the last of his hot chocolate. "Where was I? Oh, yes . . ." He **glance**d at the Askit Basket. "Mandrono!"

The basket **vanish**ed. "Just the Liophant now," he said.

Everyone looked at the Liophant, who was sitting up now in the corner, **scratch**ing behind his lion ears with his elephant **trunk**. Stanley **pat**ted him, and the Liophant **lick**ed his hand.

"How sweet!" Mrs. Lambchop said.

"George, perhaps. . . ?"

"What makes Liophants truly happy," said the genie, "is open spaces, and the **company** of other Liophants."

"Then send him where it's like that," Stanley said bravely, patting again. The Liophant vanished **halfway** through the pat.

For a moment no one spoke.

"Good for you, Stanley," Mr. Lambchop said softly. "And now you must think of a last wish to make."

While Stanley thought, Mrs. Lambchop collected the hot chocolate cups. "Where will you go now, Prince Haraz?" she said.

"Back into that **stuffy** little lamp," said the genie. "And then it's wait, wait, wait!

Hundreds and hundreds of years, probably. It's my **punish**ment for playing too many **trick**s. My friends warned me, but I wouldn't listen."

He sighed. "Mosef, Ali, Ben Sifa, little Fawz. Such wonderful **fellow**s! I think of them when I'm alone in the lamp, the *fun* they must be having. The games, the freedom. . . ." His voice **trembled**, and the Lambchops felt very sorry for him.

Suddenly, Arthur had an idea. He **whisper**ed it to Stanley.

"Why the whispering?" the genie said **cross**ly. "Let's have that last wish, Stanley, and I'll smoke back into my lamp."

The brothers were smiling at each other. "Good idea, right?" said Arthur.

"Oh, yes!" Stanley turned to the genie. "Here is my last wish, Prince Haraz. I wish for you *not* to stay in the lamp, but to go back where you came from, to be with your genie friends and have good times with them, forever from now on!"

Prince Haraz **gasp**ed. His mouth fell open.

Mr. Lambchop worried that he might **faint**. "Are you all right?" he asked. "Is Stanley not allowed to set you free?"

"Yes, yes . . . it's allowed." The genie spoke softly. "But nobody ever used a wish for the **sake** of a genie. Not until now."

"How **selfish** people can be!" said Mrs. Lambchop.

Prince Haraz **rub**bed his eyes. "What

a fine family this is," he said, beginning to smile. "I thank you all. The name of Lambchop will be **honor**ed always, wherever genies meet."

His smile enormous now, he shook hands with each of the Lambchops. The last shake was with Stanley, and the genie was already a bit **smoky** about the **edge**s. By the time he let go of Stanley's hand, he was all smoke, a dark cloud that **swirl**ed **brief**ly over the little lamp on the desk, then **pour**ed in through the **spout** until not a **puff** remained.

Full of wonder, the Lambchops **gather**ed about the lamp, and after a moment Arthur put his lips to the spout.

"Good-bye, Prince Haraz!" he called.

"Have a nice trip!"

From within the lamp, a faraway voice called back, "**Bless** you all. . . ." And then there was only silence in the room.

Mr. Lambchop was the first to speak. "I'm proud of you, Stanley," he said. "Your last wish was **generous** and kind."

"It was my idea, actually," Arthur said, and Mrs. Lambchop kissed the top of his head. "Off to bed now, boys," she said. "Tomorrow is another day."

Stanley and Arthur got into bed, and she turned out the light.

"The lamp was supposed to be a surprise birthday present," Stanley said sleepily. "Now it won't be a surprise at all."

"I will love it anyhow," said Mrs.

Lambchop. "And Prince Haraz was a **tremendous** surprise. Good night, my dears."

She kissed them both, and so did Mr. Lambchop, and they went out.

The brothers lay quietly in the darkness for a while, and then Stanley sighed. "I miss the Liophant a bit," he said. "But I don't mind about the **rest**."

"Me neither." Arthur **yawn**ed. "Florts, Stanley, and good night."

"Good night," Stanley said. "Collibots."

"Mandrono," **murmur**ed Arthur, and soon they were both asleep.

The End

스탠리와 요술램프

CONTENTS

미국 초등학생 사이에서 저스틴 비버보다 더 유명한 소년, 플랫 스탠리(Flat Stanley)!

『플랫 스탠리(Flat Stanley)』 시리즈는 미국 작가 제프 브라운(Jeff Brown)이 쓴 책으로, 한밤중에 몸 위로 떨어진 거대한 게시판에 눌려 납작해진(flat) 스탠리가 겪는 다양한 모험을 담고 있습니다. 플랫 스탠리는 아동 도서이지만 부모님과 선생님에게도 큰 사랑을 받으면서 출간된 지 50년이 넘은 지금까지 여러 세대를 아우르며 독자들에게 재미를 줍니다. 미국에서만 100만 부 이상 판매된 플랫 스탠리는 기존 챕터북 시리즈와 함께 플랫 스탠리의 세계 모험(Flat Stanley's Worldwide Adventures) 시리즈, 리더스북 등 다양한 형태로 출판되었고, 여러 언어로 번역되어 미국을 넘어 전 세계 독자들의 마음을 사로잡았습니다.

더불어 주인공 스탠리가 그려진 종이 인형을 만들어 이를 우편으로 원하는 사람에게 보내는 플랫 스탠리 프로젝트가 1995년부터 시작되면서 이 책은 더 많은 관심을 받게 되었습니다. 유명 연예인은 물론이고, 심지어 오바마 대통령까지 이 종이 인형과 함께 있는 사진을 찍어 공유하는 모습을 통해 그 인기를 짐작할 수 있습니다.

이러한 플랫 스탠리 시리즈는 한국에서도 널리 알려져 '엄마표 영어'를 하는 부모님과 초보 영어 학습자라면 반드시 읽어야 하는 영어원서로 자리 잡았습니다. 렉사일 지수가 최대 640L인 플랫 스탠리는 간결하지만, 필수적인 어휘로 쓰여져 원서 읽기에 두려움을 갖는 학습자에게도 영어로 책을 읽는 재미를 선사할 것입니다.

번역과 단어장이 포함된 워크북, 그리고 오디오북까지 담긴 풀 패키지!

이 책은 이렇게 큰 사랑을 받고 있는 영어원서 『플랫 스탠리』 시리즈에, 더욱 탁월한 학습 효과를 거둘 수 있도록 다양한 콘텐츠를 덧붙인 책입니다.

- 영어원서: 본문에 나온 어려운 어휘에 볼드 처리가 되어 있어 단어를 더욱 분명히 인지하며 자연스럽게 암기하게 됩니다.
- 단어장: 원서에 나온 어려운 어휘가 '한영'은 물론 '영영' 의미까지 완벽하게 정리되어 있으며, 반복되는 단어까지 넣어두어 자연스럽게 복습이 되도록 구성했습니다.

- 번역: 영어와 비교할 수 있도록 직역에 가까운 번역을 담았습니다. 원서 읽기에 익숙하지 않는 초보 학습자들도 어려움 없이 내용을 파악할 수 있습니다.
- 퀴즈: 매 챕터별로 내용을 확인하는 이해력 점검 퀴즈가 들어있습니다.
- 오디오북: 빠른 속도의 듣기 훈련용 오디오북(분당 약 145단어)과 천천히 녹음된 따라 읽기용 오디오북(분당 약 110단어)을 포함하고 있어 듣기 훈련은 물론 소리 내어 읽기에까지 폭넓게 사용할 수 있습니다.

이 책의 수준과 타깃 독자
- 미국 원어민 기준: 유치원 ~ 초등학교 저학년
- 한국 학습자 기준: 초등학교 저학년 ~ 중학교 1학년
- 영어원서 완독 경험이 없는 초보 영어 학습자 (토익 기준 450~750점대)
- 비슷한 수준의 다른 챕터북: Arthur Chapter Book, The Zack Files, Magic Tree House, Marvin Redpost
- 도서 분량: 약 5,900단어

플랫 스탠리, 이렇게 읽어보세요!

- **단어 암기는 이렇게!** 처음 리딩을 시작하기 전, 해당 챕터에 나오는 단어들을 눈으로 쭉 훑어봅니다. 모르는 단어는 좀 더 주의 깊게 보되, 손으로 써가면서 완벽하게 암기할 필요는 없습니다. 본문을 읽으면서 이 단어들을 다시 만나게 되는데, 그 과정에서 단어의 쓰임새와 어감을 자연스럽게 익히게 됩니다. 이렇게 책을 읽은 후에, 단어를 다시 한번 복습하세요. 복습할 때는 중요하다고 생각하는 단어들을 손으로 써가면서 꼼꼼하게 외우는 것도 좋습니다. 이런 방식으로 책을 읽다보면, 많은 단어를 빠르고 부담 없이 익히게 됩니다.

- **리딩할 때는 리딩에만 집중하자!** 원서를 읽는 중간 중간 모르는 단어가 나온다고 워크북을 들춰보거나, 곧바로 번역을 찾아보는 것은 매우 좋지 않은 습관입니다. 모르는 단어나 이해가 가지 않는 문장이 나온다고 해도 펜으로 가볍게 표시만 해두고, 전체적인 맥락을 잡아가며 빠르게 읽어나가세요. 리딩을 할 때는 속도에 대한 긴장감을 잃지 않으면서 리딩에만 집중하는 것이 좋습니다. 모르는 단어와 문장은, 리딩이 끝난 후에 한꺼번에 정리해보는 '리뷰'시간을

갖습니다. 리뷰를 할 때는 번역은 물론 단어장과 사전도 꼼꼼하게 확인하면서 왜 이해가 되지 않았는지 확인해 봅니다.

- **번역 활용은 이렇게!** 이해가 가지 않는 문장은 번역을 통해서 그 의미를 파악할 수 있습니다. 하지만 한국어와 영어는 정확히 1:1 대응이 되지 않기 때문에 번역을 활용하는 데에도 지혜가 필요합니다. 의역이 된 부분까지 억지로 의미를 대응해서 암기하려고 하기보다, 어떻게 그런 의미가 만들어진 것인지 추측하면서 번역은 참고자료로 활용하는 것이 좋습니다.

- **듣기 훈련은 이렇게!** 리스닝 실력을 향상시키길 원한다면 오디오북을 적극적으로 활용하세요. 처음에는 오디오북을 틀어놓고 눈으로 해당 내용을 따라 읽으면서 훈련을 하고, 이것이 익숙해지면 오디오북만 틀어놓고 '귀를 통해' 책을 읽어보세요. 눈으로는 한 번도 읽지 않은 책을 귀를 통해 완벽하게 이해할 수 있다면 이후에는 영어 듣기로 고생하는 일은 거의 없을 것입니다.

- **소리 내어 읽고 녹음하자!** 이 책은 특히 소리 내어 읽기(Voice Reading)에 최적화된 문장 길이와 구조를 가지고 있습니다. 또한 오디오북 CD에 포함된 '따라 읽기용' 오디오북으로 소리 내어 읽기 훈련을 함께할 수 있습니다. 소리 내어 읽기를 하면서 내가 읽은 것을 녹음하고 들어보세요! 자신의 영어 발음을 들어보는 것은 몹시 민망한 일이지만, 그 과정을 통해서 의식적·무의식적으로 발음을 교정하게 됩니다. 이렇게 영어로 소리를 만들어 본 경험은 이후 탄탄한 스피킹 실력의 밑거름이 될 것입니다.

- **2~3번 반복해서 읽자!** 영어 초보자라면 2~3회 반복해서 읽을 것을 추천합니다. 초보자일수록 처음 읽을 때는 생소한 단어들과 스토리 때문에 내용 파악에 급급할 수밖에 없습니다. 하지만 일단 내용을 파악한 후에 다시 읽으면 어휘와 문장 구조 등 다른 부분까지 관찰하면서 조금 더 깊이 있게 읽을 수 있고, 그 과정에서 리딩 속도도 빨라지고 리딩 실력을 더 확고하게 다지게 됩니다.

- **'시리즈'로 꾸준히 읽자!** 한 작가의 책을 시리즈로 읽는 것 또한 영어 실력 향상에 큰 도움이 됩니다. 같은 등장인물이 다시 나오기 때문에 내용 파악이 더 수

월할 뿐 아니라, 작가가 사용하는 어휘와 표현들도 자연스럽게 반복되기 때문에 탁월한 복습 효과까지 얻을 수 있습니다. 『플랫 스탠리』 시리즈는 현재 6권, 총 35,700단어 분량이 출간되어 있습니다. 시리즈를 꾸준히 읽다 보면 영어 실력도 자연스럽게 향상될 것입니다.

영어원서 본문 구성

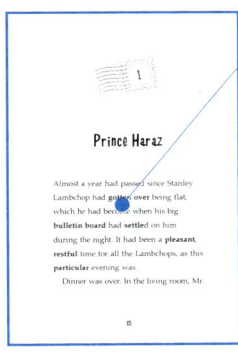

<u>내용이 담긴 본문입니다.</u>
원어민이 읽는 일반 원서와 같은 텍스트지만, 암기해야 할 중요 어휘들은 볼드체로 표시되어 있습니다. 이 어휘들은 지금 들고 계신 워크북에 챕터별로 정리되어 있습니다.

학습 심리학 연구 결과에 따르면, 한 단어씩 따로 외우는 단어 암기는 거의 효과가 없다고 합니다. 대신 단어를 제대로 외우기 위해서는 문맥(Context) 속에서 단어를 암기해야 하며, 한 단어 당 문맥 속에서 15번 이상 마주칠 때 완벽하게 암기할 수 있다고 합니다.

이 책의 본문은 중요 어휘를 볼드로 강조하여, 문맥 속의 단어들을 더 확실히 인지(Word Cognition in Context)하도록 돕고 있습니다. 또한 대부분의 중요한 단어들은 다른 챕터에서도 반복해서 등장하기 때문에 이 책을 읽는 것만으로도 자연스럽게 어휘력을 향상시킬 수 있습니다.

또한 본문에는 내용 이해를 돕기 위해 <u>'각주'가 첨가되어 있습니다.</u> 각주는 굳이 암기할 필요는 없지만, 알아두면 내용을 더 깊이 있게 이해할 수 있어 원서를 읽는 재미가 배가됩니다.

7

워크북(Workbook)의 구성

Check Your Reading Speed
해당 챕터의 단어 수가 기록되어 있어, 리딩 속도를 측정할 수 있습니다. 특히 리딩 속도를 중시하는 독자들이 유용하게 사용할 수 있습니다.

Build Your Vocabulary
본문에 볼드 표시되어 있는 단어들이 정리되어 있습니다. 리딩 전, 후에 반복해서 보면 원서를 더욱 쉽게 읽을 수 있고, 어휘력도 빠르게 향상됩니다.

단어는 〈빈도 – 스펠링 – 발음기호 – 품사 – 한글 뜻 – 영문 뜻〉 순서로 표기되어 있으며 빈도 표시(★)가 많을수록 필수 어휘입니다. 반복 등장하는 단어는 빈도 대신 '복습'으로 표기되어 있습니다. 품사는 아래와 같이 표기했습니다.

n. 명사 | a. 형용사 | ad. 부사 | v. 동사
conj. 접속사 | prep. 전치사 | int. 감탄사 | idiom 숙어 및 관용구

Comprehension Quiz
간단한 퀴즈를 통해 읽은 내용에 대한 이해력을 점검해 볼 수 있습니다.

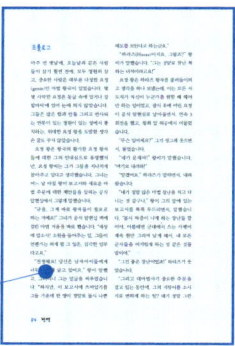

번역
영문과 비교할 수 있도록 최대한 직역에 가까운 번역을 담았습니다.

오디오북 CD 구성

이 책은 '듣기 훈련'과 '소리 내어 읽기 훈련'을
위한 2가지 종류의 오디오북이 포함되어 있습
니다.

- 듣기 훈련용 오디오북: 분당 145단어 속도
- 소리 내어 읽기 훈련용 오디오북: 분당 110
  단어 속도

오디오북은 MP3 파일로 제공되는 MP3 기기나
컴퓨터에 옮겨서 사용하셔야 합니다. 오디오북
에 이상이 있을 경우 helper@longtailbooks.co.kr
로 메일을 주시면 자세한 안내를 받으실 수 있습니다.

Prologue

1. Where did the wicked genies live?

    A. They lived in the king's palace.

    B. They lived in the tallest towers of the magical kingdom.

    C. They lived in dark forests far away from the palace.

    D. They lived in caves or deep in the rivers.

2. What did the Genie Queen think of the genie princes?

    A. She thought they were out of control.

    B. She thought they were very patient.

    C. She thought they were too serious.

    D. She thought they were old enough to grant wishes.

3. **How did the Genie King summon Prince Haraz?**

   A. He used a magic spell to make Prince Haraz appear.

   B. He told the Magic Mirror to find Prince Haraz.

   C. He sent a messenger to go and get Prince Haraz.

   D. He sent a thought to Prince Haraz.

4. **Why did the King want to speak with Prince Haraz?**

   A. Prince Haraz had taken the King's wand.

   B. Prince Haraz had been playing many jokes on others.

   C. The King wanted Prince Haraz to tell him a joke.

   D. The King wanted to ask Prince Haraz for advice.

5. **Why did the King send Prince Haraz into the lamp?**

   A. The King needed someone to look after the lamp.

   B. The King wanted to give Prince Haraz an important job.

   C. Prince Haraz had played a mean joke on the Queen.

   D. Prince Haraz had made the King feel sorry.

1분에 몇 단어를 읽는지 리딩 속도를 측정해보세요.

$$\frac{464 \ words}{reading \ time \ (\qquad) \ sec} \times 60 = (\qquad) \ WPM$$

Build Your Vocabulary

★**magical** [mǽdʒikəl] a. 마력이 있는; 마법에 쓰이는; 황홀한, 아주 멋진
Something that is magical seems to use magic or to be able to produce magic.

★**kingdom** [kíŋdəm] n. 왕국
A kingdom is a country or region that is ruled by a king or queen.

‡**importance** [impɔ́:rtəns] n. 중요성
The importance of something is its quality of being significant, valued, or necessary in a particular situation.

‡**friendly** [fréndli] a. (행동이) 친절한, 우호적인; 상냥한, 다정한
If someone is friendly, they behave in a pleasant, kind way, and like to be with other people.

★**wicked** [wíkid] a. 못된, 사악한; 짓궂은, 장난기 있는
You use wicked to describe someone or something that is very bad and deliberately harmful to people.

‡**sight** [sait] n. 시야; 광경, 모습; 보기, 봄; v. 갑자기 보다
(out of sight idiom 보이지 않는 곳에)
If something is out of sight, you cannot see it.

★**cave** [keiv] n. 동굴
A cave is a large hole in the side of a cliff or hill, or one that is under the ground.

bottom [bátəm] n. 바닥; (아래쪽) 뒷면; 맨 아래 (부분)
The bottom of something is the lowest or deepest part of it.

provoke [prəvóuk] v. 화나게 하다, 도발하다; 유발하다
If you provoke someone, you deliberately annoy them and try to make them behave aggressively.

rule [ru:l] v. 통치하다, 다스리다, 지배하다; n. 규칙; 통치, 지배
The person or group that rules a country controls its affairs.

palace [pǽlis] n. 궁전; 왕실
A palace is a very large impressive house, especially one which is the official home of a king, queen, or president.

courtyard [kɔ́:rtjàːrd] n. 안뜰, 안마당
A courtyard is an open area of ground which is surrounded by buildings or walls.

reflect [riflékt] v. (상을) 비추다; 반사하다; 깊이 생각하다
When something is reflected in a mirror or in water, you can see its image in the mirror or in the water.

pool [pu:l] n. 웅덩이; v. (자금·정보 등을) 모으다; 고이다
A pool of liquid or light is a small area of it on the ground or on a surface.

noted [nóutid] a. 유명한, 잘 알려져 있는
To be noted for something you do or have means to be well-known and admired for it.

patient [péiʃənt] a. 참을성 있는, 인내심 있는; n. 환자 (patience n. 참을성, 인내심)
If you have patience, you are able to stay calm and not get annoyed.

high-spirited [hai-spíritid] a. 활기찬, 활발한
Someone who is high-spirited is very lively and easily excited.

throne [θroun] n. 왕좌, 옥좌; 왕위, 보위 (throne room n. 공식 알현실)
A throne is a decorative chair used by a king, queen, or emperor on important official occasions.

: report [ripɔ́:rt] n. 기록, 보고; 보도;
v. (신문·방송에서) 보도하다; 알리다, 발표하다, 전하다
If you give someone a report on something, you tell them what has been happening.

: propose [prəpóuz] v. 제안하다; 작정하다; 청혼하다 (proposal n. 제안, 제의)
A proposal is a plan or an idea, often a formal or written one, which is suggested for people to think about and decide upon.

٠ spell [spel] n. 주문; 마법; v. (어떤 단어의) 철자를 말하다; 철자를 맞게 쓰다
A spell is a situation in which events are controlled by a magical power.

: discipline [dísəplin] n. 규율, 훈육; 단련법; v. 징계하다; 훈육하다
Discipline is the practice of making people obey rules or standards of behavior, and punishing them when they do not.

: adjust [ədʒʌ́st] v. (매무새 등을) 바로잡다; 조정하다; 적응하다
If you adjust something such as your clothing or a machine, you correct or alter its position or setting.

: grant [grænt] v. 승인하다, 허락하다; 인정하다; n. 보조금
If someone in authority grants you something, or if something is granted to you, you are allowed to have it.

be hard on idiom ~을 심하게 대하다
If you are hard on someone, you treat them severely or unkindly.

٠ lad [læd] n. 사내애; 청년
A lad is a young man or boy.

٠ frown [fraun] v. 얼굴을 찡그리다; 눈살을 찌푸리다; n. 찡그림, 찌푸림
When someone frowns, their eyebrows become drawn together, because they are annoyed or puzzled.

smarty [smá:rti] n. 잘난 체하는 놈
If you describe someone as a smarty, you dislike the fact that they think they are very clever and always have an answer for everything.

* **summon** [sʌ́mən] v. 호출하다, (오라고) 부르다; 소환하다
If you summon someone, you order them to come to you.

* **ruler** [rúːlər] n. 통치자, 지배자; 자
The ruler of a country is the person who rules the country.

* **flip** [flip] n. 공중제비; 톡 던지기; v. 톡 던지다; 홱 뒤집다, 휙 젖히다
(triple flip n. 3회전 공중제비)
If you do a flip, you jump up and turn completely over in the air.

* **hover** [hʌ́vər] v. (허공을) 맴돌다; 서성이다; 주저하다; n. 공중을 떠다님
To hover means to stay in the same position in the air without moving forward or backward.

‡ **grin** [grin] v. 활짝 웃다; n. 활짝 웃음
When you grin, you smile broadly.

‡ **land** [lænd] v. (땅·표면에) 내려앉다, 착륙하다; (땅에) 떨어지다; n. 육지, 땅; 지역
When someone or something lands, they come down to the ground after moving through the air or falling.

‡ **joke** [dʒouk] n. 농담; 웃음거리; v. 농담하다; 농담 삼아 말하다
A joke is something that is said or done to make you laugh, for example a funny story.

* **tap** [tæp] v. (가볍게) 톡톡 두드리다; 이용하다; n. (가볍게) 두드리기
If you tap something, you hit it with a quick light blow or a series of quick light blows.

‡ **annoy** [ənɔ́i] v. 짜증나게 하다; 귀찮게 하다 (annoying a. 짜증스러운)
Someone or something that is annoying makes you feel fairly angry and impatient.

* **carpet** [káːrpit] n. 카펫, 양탄자; v. 카펫을 깔다
A carpet is a thick covering of soft material which is laid over a floor or a staircase.

circle [sə:rkl] n. 원형; v. 빙빙 돌다; 에워싸다, 둘러싸다
A circle is a shape consisting of a curved line completely surrounding an area.

dizzy [dízi] a. 어지러운; (너무 변화가 심해) 아찔한
If you feel dizzy, you feel that you are losing your balance and are about to fall.

chief [ʧi:f] a. (계급·직급상) 최고위자인; n. (조직·집단의) 장(長)
Chief is used in the job titles of the most senior worker or workers of a particular kind in an organization.

wizard [wízərd] n. (동화 등에 나오는 남자) 마법사
In legends and fairy stories, a wizard is a man who has magic powers.

wand [wand] n. (마술사의) 지팡이
A magic wand or a wand is a long thin rod that magicians and fairies wave when they are performing tricks and magic.

cast [kæst] v. (마법 등을) 걸다; (그림자를) 드리우다; (시선·미소 등을) 던지다; n. 출연자들
To cast a magical spell means to cause it to take effect.

major [méidʒər] a. 주요한, 중대한; 심각한
You use major when you want to describe something that is more important, serious, or significant than other things in a group or situation.

shameful [ʃéimfəl] a. 수치스러운, 창피한, 부끄러운
If you describe a person's action or attitude as shameful, you think that it is so bad that the person ought to be ashamed.

severe [sivíər] a. (처벌이) 가혹한; 극심한, 심각한; 엄한 (severely ad. 심하게, 엄하게)
Severe punishments or criticisms are very strong or harsh.

punish [pʌ́niʃ] v. 처벌하다, 벌주다; (형벌·형에) 처하다
To punish someone means to make them suffer in some way because they have done something wrong.

dear [diər] n. 여보, 당신; 얘야; int. 이런! 맙소사!; a. 사랑하는; ~에게
You can call someone dear as a sign of affection.

dumb [dʌm] a. 멍청한, 바보 같은; 말을 못 하는
If you say that something is dumb, you think that it is silly and annoying.

squirt [skwəːrt] v. (액체·가스 등을 가늘게) 찍 내뿜다; 찍 짜다; n. (액체가) 찍 나옴
If you squirt a liquid somewhere or if it squirts somewhere, the liquid comes out of a narrow opening in a thin fast stream.

whirl [hwəːrl] v. 휙 돌다; 빙빙 돌다; n. 빙빙 돌기
If something or someone whirls around or if you whirl them around, they move around or turn around very quickly.

responsible [rispánsəbl] a. (~에 대해) 책임이 있는; 책임감 있는; (~을) 책임지고 있는
If someone or something is responsible for a particular event or situation, they are the cause of it or they can be blamed for it.

that does it idiom 더 이상은 못 참아!
If you say 'that does it' to someone, you show that you will not tolerate something any longer.

duty [djúːti] n. 직무, 임무; (도덕적·법률적) 의무
Duty is work that you have to do for your job.

rascal [ræskl] n. 악동; 악당
If you call a man or child a rascal, you mean that they behave badly and are rude or dishonest.

Prince Haraz

1. **Why had Stanley taken an object home from the beach?**

   A. He knew it would look nice in his room.

   B. He was very fond of old teapots.

   C. He planned to give it to his mother as a gift.

   D. He wanted to sell it to a furniture shop.

2. **Why did Stanley rub the lamp?**

   A. He was going to paint over the streaks.

   B. He was going to move it off his desk.

   C. He was trying to figure out how to open it.

   D. He was trying to polish it.

3. How did Arthur feel when he saw smoke come out of the spout?

    A. He was worried that the bedroom would get dirty.

    B. He was afraid that the pot would explode.

    C. He was excited to see puffs of smoke.

    D. He was curious about what was inside the pot.

4. What was Stanley NOT allowed to wish for?

    A. He was not allowed to wish for anything cruel.

    B. He was not allowed to wish for anything fun.

    C. He was not allowed to wish for anything expensive.

    D. He was not allowed to wish for anything silly.

5. What did Mr. and Mrs. Lambchop think when Stanley told them about the lamp?

    A. They thought Stanley was telling the truth.

    B. They thought Stanley was making up a story.

    C. They thought Stanley had just finished his homework.

    D. They thought Stanley should wish for gold and diamonds.

Check Your Reading Speed

1분에 몇 단어를 읽는지 리딩 속도를 측정해보세요.

$$\frac{913 \ words}{reading \ time \ (\quad) \ sec} \times 60 = (\quad) \ WPM$$

Build Your Vocabulary

get over idiom ~을 극복하다

If you get over something, you deal with or gain control of it.

bulletin board [búlitən bɔːrd] n. 게시판

A bulletin board is a board which is usually attached to a wall in order to display notices giving information about something.

settle [setl] v. (떨어져·내려) 앉다; 자리를 잡다; 결정하다; 정착하다

If something settles or if you settle it, it sinks slowly down and becomes still.

pleasant [plézənt] a. 즐거운, 기분 좋은; 상냥한

Something that is pleasant is nice, enjoyable, or attractive.

restful [réstfəl] a. (마음이) 편안한, 평화로운

Something that is restful helps you to feel calm and relaxed.

particular [pərtíkjulər] a. 특정한; 특별한; 까다로운; n. 자세한 사실

You use particular to emphasize that you are talking about one thing or one kind of thing rather than other similar ones.

dear [diər] n. 여보, 당신; 얘야; int. 이런, 맙소사!; a. 사랑하는; ~에게

You can call someone dear as a sign of affection.

darn [dɑːrn] v. 꿰매다, 짜깁다

If you darn a hole or a piece of clothing, you repair it with long stitches across the hole and other stitches across them.

20

company [kˈʌmpəni] n. 함께 있음; 회사; 단체
Company is having another person or other people with you, usually when this is pleasant or stops you feeling lonely.

excuse [ikskjúːz] n. 핑계 거리; 변명, 이유; v. 용서하다
An excuse is a reason which you give in order to explain why something has been done or has not been done, or in order to avoid doing something.

chuckle [ʧˈʌkl] v. 킬킬 웃다; 빙그레 웃다; n. 킬킬거림; 속으로 웃기
When you chuckle, you laugh quietly.

imaginative [imǽdʒənətiv] a. 창의적인, 상상력이 풍부한
If you describe someone or their ideas as imaginative, you are praising them because they are easily able to think of or create new or exciting things.

pajamas [pədʒáːməz] n. (바지와 상의로 된) 잠옷
A pair of pajamas consists of loose trousers and a loose jacket that people, especially men, wear in bed.

mighty [máiti] a. 강력한, 힘센; ad. 대단히, 굉장히
Mighty is used to describe something that is very large or powerful.

concentrate [kˈɑnsəntrèit] v. (정신을) 집중하다; (한 곳에) 모으다; n. 농축물
If you concentrate on something, or concentrate your mind on it, you give all your attention to it.

pot [pat] n. 그릇; 냄비; 항아리; v. (나무를) 화분에 심다 (teapot n. 찻주전자)
A teapot is a container with a lid, a handle, and a spout, used for making and serving tea.

squash [skwaʃ] v. 찌부러뜨리다, 짓누르다; (좁은 곳에) 밀어 넣다
If someone or something is squashed, they are pressed or crushed with such force that they become injured or lose their shape.

curve [kəːrv] v. 곡선으로 나아가다, 곡선을 이루다; n. 곡선
If something curves, or if someone or something curves it, it has the shape of a curve.

spout [spaut] n. (주전자 등의) 주둥이; (액체의) 분출; v. (액체를) 내뿜다
A spout is a long, hollow part of a container through which liquids can be poured out easily.

knob [nab] n. (동그란) 손잡이; 혹, 마디
A knob is a round handle on a door or drawer which you use in order to open or close it.

wave [weiv] n. 파도, 물결; (손·팔을) 흔들기; v. (손·팔을) 흔들다; 흔들리다
A wave is a raised mass of water on the surface of water, especially the sea.

roll [roul] v. 굴리다; 뒹굴다; (동글게) 말다; n. 통, 두루마리; 뒹굴기; 구르기
When something rolls or when you roll it, it moves along a surface, turning over many times.

fond [fand] a. 좋아하는; 다정한, 애정 어린
If you are fond of something, you like it or you like doing it very much.

furniture [fə́ːrniʧər] n. 가구
Furniture consists of large objects such as tables, chairs, or beds that are used in a room for sitting or lying on or for putting things on or in.

silverware [sílvərwɛər] n. 은제품, 은식기류
You can use silverware to refer to all the things in a house that are made of silver, especially the cutlery and dishes.

streak [striːk] n. 줄무늬; v. 전속력으로 가다; 기다란 자국을 내다
A streak is a long stripe or mark on a surface which contrasts with the surface because it is a different color.

brownish [bráuniʃ] a. 약간 갈색인, 갈색을 띠는
Something that is brownish is slightly brown in color.

polish [páliʃ] v. (윤이 나도록) 닦다, 광을 내다; n. 닦기; 세련
If you polish something, you put polish on it or rub it with a cloth to make it shine.

‡ **rub** [rʌb] v. (손·손수건 등을 대고) 문지르다; (두 손 등을) 맞비비다; n. 문지르기, 비비기
If you rub an object or a surface, you move a cloth backward and forward over it in order to clean or dry it.

⋆ **sleeve** [sli:v] n. (옷의) 소매
The sleeves of a coat, shirt, or other item of clothing are the parts that cover your arms.

⋆ **puff** [pʌf] n. 훅 부는 소리; (공기·연기 등의) 작은 양;
v. (많은 양의 연기·김을) 내뿜다; 부풀어오르다
A puff of something such as air or smoke is a small amount of it that is blown out from somewhere.

yipe [jaip] int. 에그머니!, 아이구!
You can use yipe as an expression of surprise, fear, or pain.

⋆ **explode** [iksplóud] v. 폭발하다; 폭발적으로 증가하다; 갑자기 ~하다
If an object such as a bomb explodes or if someone or something explodes it, it bursts loudly and with great force, often causing damage or injury.

‡ **rapid** [ræpid] a. (속도가) 빠른; (행동이) 민첩한 (rapidly ad. 빠르게, 신속히)
A rapid movement is one that is very fast.

look out idiom 조심해라!
If you say 'Look out!' to someone, you tell them to be careful, especially when there is some danger.

swirl [swə:rl] v. 소용돌이치다, 빙빙 돌다; n. 소용돌이
If you swirl something liquid or flowing, or if it swirls, it moves round and round quickly.

⋆ **mixture** [míkstʃər] n. 혼합물; 섞기, 혼합하기
A mixture of things consists of several different things together.

⋆ **slender** [sléndər] a. 날씬한, 호리호리한; 가느다란; (양·크기가) 얼마 안 되는
A slender person is attractively thin and graceful.

cheerful [tʃíərfəl] a. 발랄한, 쾌활한; 쾌적한
Someone who is cheerful is happy and shows this in their behavior.

hover [hʌ́vər] v. (허공을) 맴돌다; 서성이다; 주저하다; n. 공중을 떠다님
To hover means to stay in the same position in the air without moving forward or backward.

decorate [dékərèit] v. 꾸미다; 실내장식을 하다; (훈장을) 수여하다
If you decorate something, you make it more attractive by adding things to it.

loose [luːs] v. (옷이) 헐렁한; 헐거워진, 풀린; v. ~을 되는대로 늘어놓다; 느슨하게 하다
Clothes that are loose are rather large and do not fit closely.

curious [kjúəriəs] a. 별난, 특이한; 궁금한; 호기심이 많은
If you describe something as curious, you mean that it is unusual or difficult to understand.

flap [flæp] v. 펄럭거리다; (새가 날개를) 퍼덕거리다; n. 퍼덕거림; 덮개
If something such as a piece of cloth or paper flaps or if you flap it, it moves quickly up and down or from side to side.

trousers [tráuzərz] n. 바지
Trousers are a piece of clothing that you wear over your body from the waist downward, and that cover each leg separately.

snag [snæg] v. (날카롭거나 튀어나온 것에) 걸리다; 잡아 채다; n. (작은·예상 밖의) 문제
If you snag part of your clothing on a sharp or rough object or if it snags, it gets caught on the object and tears.

scary [skéəri] a. 무서운, 겁나는
Something that is scary is rather frightening.

float [flout] v. (물 위나 공중에서) 떠가다; (물에) 뜨다; n. 부표
Something that floats in or through the air hangs in it or moves slowly and gently through it.

* **bow** [bau] v. (허리를 굽혀) 절하다; (고개를) 숙이다; n. (고개 숙여 하는) 인사
When you bow to someone, you briefly bend your body toward them as a formal way of greeting them or showing respect.

drop in idiom 잠깐 들르다
To drop in means to pay a short, informal visit to someone, often without arranging this in advance.

* **gasp** [gæsp] v. 숨이 턱 막히다; 헉 하고 숨을 쉬다; 숨을 제대로 못 쉬다; n. 헉 하는 소리를 냄
When you gasp, you take a short quick breath through your mouth, especially when you are surprised, shocked, or in pain.

: **dive** [daiv] v. (dived/dove–dived) 급히 움직이다; (물 속으로) 뛰어들다; 급강하다;
n. (물 속으로) 뛰어들기
If you dive in a particular direction or into a particular place, you jump or move there quickly.

복습 **friendly** [fréndli] a. (행동이) 친절한, 우호적인; 상냥한, 다정한
If someone is friendly, they behave in a pleasant, kind way, and like to be with other people.

coop up idiom (좁은 곳에) 가두다
If a person or animal is cooped up in a place, they have to stay there without being able to move around much.

: **knee** [niː] n. 무릎; v. 무릎으로 치다
Your knee is the place where your leg bends.

: **chin** [ʧin] n. 턱
Your chin is the part of your face that is below your mouth and above your neck.

by accident idiom 우연히
If something happens by accident, it happens completely by chance.

turn into idiom ～이 되다, ～으로 변하다
To turn or be turned into something means to change, or to make a thing change, into something different.

‡ **scare** [skɛər] v. 겁주다, 놀라게 하다; 무서워하다; n. 불안(감); 놀람, 공포
(scared a. 무서워하는, 겁먹은)
If you are scared of someone or something, you are frightened of them.

whoosh [hwuːʃ] v. (아주 빠르게) 휙 하고 지나가다; n. 쉭 하는 소리
If something whooshes somewhere, it moves there quickly or suddenly.

복습 **grant** [grænt] v. 승인하다, 허락하다; 인정하다; n. 보조금
If someone in authority grants you something, or if something is granted to you, you are allowed to have it.

‡ **cruel** [kruːəl] a. 잔혹한, 잔인한; 고통스러운, 괴로운
Someone who is cruel deliberately causes pain or distress to people or animals.

＊ **nasty** [nǽsti] a. 못된, 심술궂은; 끔찍한, 형편없는
If you describe a person or their behavior as nasty, you mean that they behave in an unkind and unpleasant way.

‡ **jar** [dʒɑːr] n. 병; 단지; v. 불쾌감을 주다, (신경을) 거슬리다
A jar is a glass container with a lid that is used for storing food.

stinker [stíŋkər] n. 아주 기분 나쁜 인간, 골칫거리
If you describe someone or something as a stinker, you mean that you think they are very unpleasant or bad.

＊ **suspicious** [səspíʃəs] a. 의혹을 갖는, 수상쩍어 하는; 의심스러운
If you are suspicious of someone or something, you do not trust them, and are careful when dealing with them.

test out idiom ～를 시험해 보다
To test someone out means to try to find out what qualities they have or how they will react in a particular situation.

＊ **hay** [hei] n. 건초
Hay is grass which has been cut and dried so that it can be used to feed animals.

mend [mend] v. (구멍 등을) 꿰매다; 수리하다; 해결하다 (mending n. 수선; 고치는 일)
Mending is the sewing and repairing of clothes that have got holes in them.

turn out idiom ~인 것으로 드러나다; 되어 가다; 나타나다
To turn out means to be discovered or prove to be something.

treasure [tréʒər] n. 보물; 대단히 귀중한 것; v. 대단히 소중히 여기다
Treasure is a collection of valuable old objects such as gold coins and jewels that has been hidden or lost.

chest [ʧest] ① n. 상자, 궤 ② n. 가슴, 흉부
A chest is a large, heavy box used for storing things.

tax [tæks] n. 세금; v. 세금을 부과하다, 과세하다
Tax is an amount of money that you have to pay to the government so that it can pay for public services.

amuse [əmjúːz] v. 즐겁게 하다, 재미있게 하다 (amusing a. 재미있는, 즐거운)
Someone or something that is amusing makes you laugh or smile.

The Askit Basket

1. **Why did Stanley wish for an Askit Basket?**

   A. Arthur begged him to wish for it.

   B. He wished for it by mistake.

   C. He wanted to finish his homework quickly.

   D. He was wondering what an Askit Basket looked like.

2. **What did Arthur think of the English homework that Shirleen had written for him?**

   A. Arthur thought the quality of the writing was just average.

   B. Arthur thought the handwriting didn't look like his.

   C. It was exactly what Arthur had wanted.

   D. It was not what Arthur had hoped for.

3. **Why did Prince Haraz create a Liophant?**
   A. Stanley had wanted a lion that was more unique than normal lions.
   B. Stanley had wanted both a lion and an elephant as pets.
   C. Stanley had wished for a lion at first, but then he wished for an elephant.
   D. Stanley had wished for a lion that looked like an elephant.

4. **How did Stanley feel about the Liophant?**
   A. He was glad to have the Liophant.
   B. He was upset that he hadn't gotten an elephant.
   C. He felt bad about mixing up his wish.
   D. He felt sorry for the Liophant.

5. **Why did Mr. Lambchop put a note on the Askit Basket that said NOT IN USE?**
   A. The Askit Basket was broken.
   B. He wanted to use the Askit Basket for something besides homework.
   C. He planned to give the Askit Basket to someone else.
   D. He did not want Stanley and Arthur to use the Askit Basket anymore.

Check Your Reading Speed

1분에 몇 단어를 읽는지 리딩 속도를 측정해보세요.

$$\frac{1,605 \ words}{reading \ time \ (\qquad) \ sec} \times 60 = (\qquad) \ WPM$$

Build Your Vocabulary

복습 **puff** [pʌf] v. (많은 양의 연기·김을) 내뿜다; 부풀어오르다;
n. (바람·증기 등의) 훅 하는 소리; (공기·연기 등의) 작은 양
If an engine, chimney, or boiler puffs smoke or steam, clouds of smoke or steam come out of it.

복습 **pot** [pat] n. 그릇; 냄비; 항아리; v. (나무를) 화분에 심다
You can use pot to refer to a teapot or coffee pot.

: **apologize** [əpálədʒàiz] v. 사과하다
When you apologize to someone, you say that you are sorry that you have hurt them or caused trouble for them.

: **crawl** [krɔːl] v. 기다; 기어가다; 몹시 느리게 가다; n. 기어가기, 서행
When you crawl, you move forward on your hands and knees.

복습 **scary** [skέəri] a. 무서운, 겁나는
Something that is scary is rather frightening.

* **stuff** [stʌf] n. 것, 물건; v. 채워 넣다; 쑤셔 넣다
You can use stuff to refer to things such as a substance, a collection of things, events, or ideas, or the contents of something in a general way without mentioning the thing itself by name.

: **hardly** [háːrdli] ad. 거의 ~할 수가 없다; 거의 ~아니다; ~하자마자
When you say you can hardly do something, you are emphasizing that it is very difficult for you to do it.

30

stare [stɛər] v. 빤히 쳐다보다, 응시하다; n. 빤히 쳐다보기, 응시
If you stare at someone or something, you look at them for a long time.

amaze [əméiz] v. (대단히) 놀라게 하다; 경악하게 하다 (amazed a. (대단히) 놀란)
If something amazes you, it surprises you very much.

straw [strɔː] n. 짚, 밀짚; 빨대
Straw consists of the dried, yellowish stalks from crops such as wheat or barley.

decorate [dékərèit] v. 꾸미다; 실내장식을 하다; (훈장을) 수여하다
If you decorate something, you make it more attractive by adding things to it.

zigzag [zígzæg] a. Z자형의, 지그재그의; n. 지그재그; v. 지그재그로 나아가다
A zigzag is a line or pattern that looks like a Z or a row of Zs joined together.

stripe [straip] n. 줄무늬; v. 줄무늬를 넣다
A stripe is a long line which is a different color from the areas next to it.

float [flout] v. (물 위나 공중에서) 떠가다; (물에) 뜨다; n. 부표
Something that floats in or through the air hangs in it or moves slowly and gently through it.

yipe [jaip] int. 에그머니!, 아이구!
You can use yipe as an expression of surprise, fear, or pain.

silly [síli] a. 어리석은, 바보 같은; 우스꽝스러운; n. 바보
If you say that someone or something is silly, you mean that they are foolish, childish, or ridiculous.

ordinary [ɔ́ːrdənèri] a. 보통의, 평범한
Ordinary people or things are normal and not special or different in any way.

foolish [fúːliʃ] a. 바보 같은 (기분이 들게 하는); 어리석은
If you look or feel foolish, you look or feel so silly or ridiculous that people are likely to laugh at you.

‡ **lean** [liːn] v. 기울이다, (몸을) 숙이다; ~에 기대다; a. 호리호리한
When you lean in a particular direction, you bend your body in that direction.

‡ **steady** [stédi] a. 흔들림 없는, 안정된; 꾸준한; v. 흔들리지 않다, 진정되다
A steady situation continues or develops gradually without any interruptions and is not likely to change quickly.

★ **hum** [hʌm] n. 웅웅거리는 소리; v. 콧노래를 부르다, (노래를) 흥얼거리다; 웅웅거리다
A hum is a continuous low noise.

‡ **announcer** [ənáunsər] n. (프로그램) 방송 진행자
An announcer is someone who introduces programs on radio or television or who reads the text of a radio or television advertisement.

‡ **available** [əvéiləbl] a. 시간이 있는; 이용할 수 있는
Someone who is available is not busy and is therefore free to talk to you or to do a particular task.

★ **personnel** [pə̀ːrsənél] n. 직원, 인원
The personnel of an organization are the people who work for it.

★ **faraway** [fáːrəwei] a. 멀리 떨어진, 먼; 생각이 딴 데 가 있는 듯한
A faraway place is a long distance from you or from a particular place.

★ **shrug** [ʃrʌg] v. (어깨를) 으쓱하다; n. 어깨를 으쓱하기
If you shrug, you raise your shoulders to show that you are not interested in something or that you do not know or care about something.

★ **click** [klik] n. 딸깍 (하는 소리); v. 딸깍 하는 소리를 내다
A click is a short sound like the sound when you press a switch.

bouncy [báunsi] a. 활기 넘치는; 잘 튀는, 탱탱한
Someone or something that is bouncy is very lively.

‡ **cheer** [ʧiər] n. 쾌활함, 생기; 환호; v. 환호하다; 응원하다
(be of good cheer idiom 기분이 좋다)
If you are of good cheer, you are happy.

bunch [bʌnʧ] n. (양·수가) 많음; 다발, 묶음
A bunch of things is a number of things, especially a large number.

convenience [kənvíːnjəns] n. 편리, 편의
If something is done for your convenience, it is done in a way that is useful or suitable for you.

cheery [ʧíəri] a. (사람이나 그의 행동이) 쾌활한
If you describe a person or their behavior as cheery, you mean that they are cheerful and happy.

lid [lid] n. 뚜껑
A lid is the top of a box or other container which can be removed or raised when you want to open the container.

sheet [ʃiːt] n. (종이) 한 장; (침대) 시트
A sheet of paper is a rectangular piece of paper.

clear one's throat idiom 목을 가다듬다; 헛기침하다
If you clear your throat, you cough once in order to make it easier to speak or to attract people's attention.

teeny [tíːni] a. 아주 작은
If you describe something as teeny, you are emphasizing that it is very small.

handwriting [hǽndràitiŋ] n. (개인의) 필적
Your handwriting is your style of writing with a pen or pencil.

lined [laind] a. (종이가) 줄이 쳐진; 주름진
Lined paper has lines printed across it to help you write neatly.

cover [kʌ́vər] v. 덮다; 씌우다; 취재하다; n. 덮개; 몸을 숨길 곳
To cover something with or in something else means to put a layer of the second thing over its surface.

president [prézədənt] n. 대통령; 회장
The president of a country that has no king or queen is the person who is the head of state of that country.

astronaut [ǽstrənɔ̀ːt] n. 우주 비행사
An astronaut is a person who is trained for travelling in a spacecraft.

dress up idiom 잘 차려 입다
If someone is dressed up, they are wearing special clothes, in order to look smarter than usual or in order to disguise themselves.

mighty [máiti] a. 강력한, 힘센; ad. 대단히, 굉장히
Mighty is used to describe something that is very large or powerful.

extra [ékstrə] ad. 각별히, 특별히; a. 여분의, 추가의; n. 추가되는 것
You can use extra in front of adjectives and adverbs to emphasize the quality that they are describing.

pluck [plʌk] v. (잡아 당겨) 빼내다; (위험한 장소·상황에서) 구해 내다; n. 용기, 결단
If you pluck something from somewhere, you take it between your fingers and pull it sharply from where it is.

take up idiom (시간·공간을) 차지하다
To take up something means to fill a particular amount of space or time.

pet [pet] n. 애완동물; v. (동물·아이를 다정하게) 어루만지다
A pet is an animal that you keep in your home to give you company and pleasure.

leash [liːʃ] n. 가죽 끈, 사슬; 속박, 통제
A dog's leash is a long thin piece of leather or a chain, which you attach to the dog's collar so that you can keep the dog under control.

friendly [fréndli] a. (행동이) 친절한, 우호적인; 상냥한, 다정한
If someone is friendly, they behave in a pleasant, kind way, and like to be with other people.

realize [ríːəlaiz] v. 깨닫다, 알아차리다; 실현하다, 달성하다
If you realize that something is true, you become aware of that fact or understand it.

scare [skɛər] v. 겁주다, 놀라게 하다; 무서워하다; n. 불안(감); 놀람, 공포
If something scares you, it frightens or worries you.

trunk [trʌŋk] n. (코끼리의) 코; 나무의 몸통
An elephant's trunk is its very long nose that it uses to lift food and water to its mouth.

neat [niːt] a. (작고) 아기자기한; 정돈된, 단정한
A neat object, part of the body, or shape is quite small and has a smooth outline.

mane [mein] n. (말·사자 목덜미의) 갈기
The mane on a horse or lion is the long thick hair that grows from its neck.

brownish [bráuniʃ] a. 약간 갈색인, 갈색을 띠는
Something that is brownish is slightly brown in color.

tail [teil] n. (동물의) 꼬리; 끝부분; v. 미행하다
The tail of an animal, bird, or fish is the part extending beyond the end of its body.

ruff [rʌf] n. (새·동물의) 목둘레 털
A ruff is a thick band of feathers or fur round the neck of a bird or animal.

tip [tip] n. (뾰족한) 끝; v. 기울이다, 젖히다; 살짝 건드리다
The tip of something long and narrow is the end of it.

goodness [gúdnis] int. 와!, 어머나!, 맙소사!; n. 신; 선량함
People sometimes say 'my goodness' or 'goodness' to express surprise.

annoy [ənɔ́i] v. 짜증나게 하다; 귀찮게 하다 (annoyed a. 짜증이 난, 약이 오른)
If you are annoyed, you are fairly angry about something.

overlap [óuvərlæp] v. (두 가지 일이) 겹치다; n. 공통부분; 겹침
If one thing overlaps another, or if you overlap them, a part of the first thing occupies the same area as a part of the other thing.

roar [rɔːr] n. 으르렁거림, 포효; 울부짖는 듯한 소리;
v. 으르렁거리다; (크고 깊은 소리로) 울다; 고함치다
A roar is the loud deep sound that a lion makes.

snort [snɔ:rt] n. 코웃음, 콧방귀; v. 코웃음을 치다, 콧방귀를 뀌다
A snort is a sudden loud noise that you make through your nose, for example because you are angry or laughing.

growl [graul] n. 으르렁거리는 소리; v. 으르렁거리다; 으르렁거리듯 말하다
A growl is a frightening or unfriendly low noise.

honk [haŋk] n. 끼루룩 (하고 우는 소리); v. (자동차 경적을) 울리다; (기러기가) 울다
A honk is a short, loud sound made by a car horn or a goose.

hind [haind] a. 뒤쪽의, 후방의
An animal's hind legs are at the back of its body.

pant [pænt] n. 헐떡거림; v. (숨을) 헐떡이다
If you pant, you breathe quickly and loudly with your mouth open, because you have been doing something energetic.

pat [pæt] v. 쓰다듬다; 가볍게 두드리다; n. 쓰다듬기, 토닥거리기
If you pat something or someone, you tap them lightly, usually with your hand held flat.

tickle [tikl] v. 간지럽히다; 간질간질하다; n. (장난으로) 간지럽히기
When you tickle someone, you move your fingers lightly over a sensitive part of their body, often in order to make them laugh.

lick [lik] v. 핥다; 핥아먹다; n. 한 번 핥기, 핥아먹기
When people or animals lick something, they move their tongue across its surface.

mix up idiom ~을 뒤죽박죽으로 뒤섞다
If you mix up things, you change the order or arrangement of things in a confused or untidy way.

knock [nak] n. 문 두드리는 소리; 부딪침; v. 치다, 부딪치다; (문 등을) 두드리다
A knock is a sudden short noise made when someone or something hits a surface.

* **gracious** [gréiʃəs] int. 세상에!, 맙소사!; a. 자애로운; 우아한
Some people say 'gracious' or 'good gracious' in order to express surprise or annoyance.

복습 **bow** [bau] n. (고개 숙여 하는) 인사; v. (허리를 굽혀) 절하다; (고개를) 숙이다
A bow is an act of bending the head or upper body as a sign of respect or greeting.

복습 **lad** [læd] n. 사내애; 청년
A lad is a young man or boy.

‡ **generous** [dʒénərəs] a. 너그러운; 넉넉한
A generous person gives more of something, especially money, than is usual or expected.

‡ **expect** [ikspékt] v. 예상하다, 기대하다 (unexpected a. 예기치 않은, 예상 밖의)
If an event or someone's behavior is unexpected, it surprises you because you did not think that it was likely to happen.

at once idiom 즉시; 동시에
If you do something at once, you do it immediately.

복습 **dear** [diər] n. 얘야; 여보, 당신; int. 이런!, 맙소사!; a. 사랑하는; ~에게
You can call someone dear as a sign of affection.

snuffle [snʌfl] v. 코를 킁킁거리다; 코를 훌쩍이다; n. 코를 킁킁거리기
If a person or an animal snuffles, they breathe in noisily through their nose.

‡ **bowl** [boul] n. (우묵한) 그릇; 한 그릇(의 양)
A bowl is a round container with a wide uncovered top.

* **approve** [əprúːv] v. 좋다고 인정하다, 찬성하다; 승인하다
If you approve of an action, event, or suggestion, you like it or are pleased about it.

‡ **credit** [krédit] n. 칭찬; 인정; 신용; 입금; v. 입금하다; ~의 공으로 믿다
If you get the credit for something good, people praise you because you are responsible for it, or are thought to be responsible for it.

* **blush** [blʌʃ] v. 얼굴을 붉히다; ~에 부끄러워하다; n. 얼굴이 붉어짐
When you blush, your face becomes redder than usual because you are ashamed or embarrassed.

* **cardboard** [káːrdbɔːrd] n. 판지
Cardboard is thick, stiff paper that is used, for example, to make boxes and models.

* **tape** [teip] v. 테이프로 붙이다; 녹음하다, 녹화하다; n. (녹음·녹화) 테이프; (접착용) 테이프
If you tape one thing to another, you attach it using sticky tape.

⋮ **fold** [fould] v. 접다; (두 손·팔 등을) 끼다; n. 주름; 접힌 부분
If a piece of furniture or equipment folds or if you can fold it, you can make it smaller by bending or closing parts of it.

cot [kat] n. 간이 침대
A cot is a small bed that you can fold up.

* **closet** [klázit] n. 벽장
A closet is a piece of furniture with doors at the front and shelves inside, which is used for storing things.

set up idiom ~을 세우다; (기계·장비를) 설치하다
If you set up something, you build it or put it somewhere.

put out idiom (불·전깃불 등을) 끄다; 내다 놓다
If you put out a light, you make it stop shining by pressing or moving a switch.

⋮ **except** [iksépt] prep. ~을 제외하고는
You use except for to introduce the only thing or person that prevents a statement from being completely true.

* **snore** [snɔːr] v. 코를 골다; n. 코 고는 소리
When someone who is asleep snores, they make a loud noise each time they breathe.

^{복습} company [kʌ́mpəni] n. 함께 있음; 회사; 단체

Company is having another person or other people with you, usually when this is pleasant or stops you feeling lonely.

In the Park

1. **How did Mr. Lambchop introduce Prince Haraz to his friend Ralph Jones?**

   A. He introduced Prince Haraz as a relative.

   B. He introduced Prince Haraz as a friend of Arthur's.

   C. He introduced Prince Haraz as a well-known genie.

   D. He introduced Prince Haraz as a student from another country.

2. **What did Stanley do for his mother?**

   A. He made a wish for his mother to be famous.

   B. He made a wish for his mother to be a great athlete.

   C. He made a wish for his mother to meet the world's best tennis player.

   D. He made a wish for his mother to meet many foreign tourists.

3. Why was the tennis player Tom McRude at the tennis court?

   A. He was going to compete in a tennis championship.

   B. He was going to demonstrate his tennis skills.

   C. He was going to take a tennis lesson.

   D. He was going to act in a TV show.

4. How did Tom McRude treat Mr. Lambchop when he volunteered to play together?

   A. He showed Mr. Lambchop a lot of patience.

   B. He showed Mr. Lambchop respect.

   C. He was unkind to Mr. Lambchop.

   D. He was fair to Mr. Lambchop.

5. What did the Lambchops see on the evening news?

   A. They saw Tom McRude signing autographs.

   B. They saw Mrs. Lambchop giving a short statement.

   C. They saw Mr. Lambchop playing tennis.

   D. They saw Prince Haraz granting wishes.

Check Your Reading Speed

1분에 몇 단어를 읽는지 리딩 속도를 측정해보세요.

$$\frac{1,673 \text{ words}}{\text{reading time ( ) sec}} \times 60 = (\quad) \text{ WPM}$$

Build Your Vocabulary

particular [pərtíkjulər] a. 특별한; 특정한; 까다로운; n. 자세한 사실
(particularly ad. 특히, 특별히)
You use particularly to indicate that what you are saying applies especially to one thing or situation.

loaf [louf] n. (pl. loaves) 빵 한 덩이; v. 빈둥거리다
A loaf of bread is bread which has been shaped and baked in one piece.

set out idiom (여행을) 시작하다; ~을 진열하다
If you set out, you leave a place and begin a journey, especially a long journey.

racket [rǽkit] n. (테니스 등의) 라켓; 시끄러운 소리, 소음
A racket is an oval-shaped bat with strings across it. Rackets are used in tennis, squash, and badminton.

court [kɔːrt] n. (테니스 등을 하는) 코트; 법정, 법원
A court is an area in which you play a game such as tennis, basketball, badminton, or squash.

aware [əwéər] a. 알고 있는, 자각하고 있는; 눈치 채고 있는
If you are aware of something, you know about it.

puzzle [pʌzl] v. 어리둥절하게 하다; n. 퍼즐; 수수께끼
If something puzzles you, you do not understand it and feel confused.

slacks [slæks] n. 바지
Slacks are a casual pair of pants.

college [kálidʒ] n. 대학(교)
A college is an institution where students study for degrees and where academic research is done.

run into idiom ~와 우연히 만나다, 마주치다
If you run into someone, you meet them by chance.

round [raund] v. 둥글게 만들다; (모퉁이·커브 등을) 돌다; a. 둥근, 동그란
If you round something, you make it into a shape like a circle or ball.

foreign [fɔ́ːrən] a. 외국의; 대외의
Something or someone that is foreign comes from or relates to a country that is not your own.

remark [rimáːrk] v. 언급하다, 말하다; n. 발언, 언급; 주목
If you remark that something is the case, you say that it is the case.

amaze [əméiz] v. (대단히) 놀라게 하다; 경악하게 하다 (amazed a. (대단히) 놀란)
If something amazes you, it surprises you very much.

gracious [gréiʃəs] int. 세상에!, 맙소사!; a. 자애로운; 우아한
Some people say 'gracious' or 'good gracious' in order to express surprise or annoyance.

nevertheless [nèvərðəlés] ad. 그렇기는 하지만, 그럼에도 불구하고
You use nevertheless when saying something that contrasts with what has just been said.

questioning [kwésʧəniŋ] a. 의문을 나타내는, 묻고 싶은 듯한; n. 질의, 심문
If someone has a questioning expression on their face, they look as if they want to know the answer to a question.

nod [nad] n. (고개를) 끄덕임; v. (고개를) 끄덕이다, 까딱하다
A nod is a movement up and down with the head.

lecture [lékʧər] v. 강의하다; 잔소리를 하다; n. 강의, 강연; 설교
If you lecture on a particular subject, you give a talk to a group of people about it.

passenger [pǽsəndʒər] n. 승객
A passenger in a vehicle such as a bus, boat, or plane is a person who is travelling in it, but who is not driving it or working on it.

megaphone [mégəfoun] n. 확성기
A megaphone is a cone-shaped device for making your voice sound louder in the open air.

announce [ənáuns] v. 발표하다, 알리다; 선언하다
If you announce something, you tell people about it publicly or officially.

statue [stǽʧuː] n. 조각상
A statue is a large sculpture of a person or an animal, made of stone or metal.

folk [fouk] n. (pl.) 여러분, 얘들아; (pl.) (일반적인) 사람들; (pl.) 부모
You can use folks as a term of address when you are talking to several people.

in person idiom 직접, 몸소
If you do something in person, you do it yourself rather than letting someone else do it for you.

pleased [pliːzd] a. 기쁜, 기뻐하는, 만족해하는
If you are pleased, you are happy about something or satisfied with something.

astonish [əstániʃ] v. 깜짝 놀라게 하다 (astonishment n. 깜짝 놀람)
Astonishment is a feeling of great surprise.

stare [stɛər] v. 빤히 쳐다보다, 응시하다; n. 빤히 쳐다보기, 응시
If you stare at someone or something, you look at them for a long time.

goodness [gúdnis] int. 와!, 어머나!, 맙소사!; n. 신; 선량함
People sometimes say 'my goodness' or 'goodness' to express surprise.

44

‡ **rush** [rʌʃ] v. 급히 움직이다; 서두르다; 재촉하다; n. 혼잡, 분주함
If you rush somewhere, you go there quickly.

‡ **reach** [riːʧ] v. ~에 이르다; (손·팔을) 뻗다; n. (닿을 수 있는) 거리; 범위
When someone or something reaches a place, they arrive there.

복습 **bow** [bau] v. (허리를 굽혀) 절하다; (고개를) 숙이다; n. (고개 숙여 하는) 인사
When you bow to someone, you briefly bend your body toward them
as a formal way of greeting them or showing respect.

‡ **polite** [pəláit] a. 예의 바른, 공손한; 의례적인 (politely ad. 예의 바르게, 점잖게)
Someone who is polite has good manners and behaves in a way that is
socially correct and not rude to other people.

‡ **honor** [ánər] n. 영광(스러운 것); 존경, 공경; v. 존경하다; 수여하다
If you describe doing or experiencing something as an honor, you mean
you think it is something special and desirable.

복습 **grant** [grænt] v. 승인하다, 허락하다; 인정하다; n. 보조금
If someone in authority grants you something, or if something is granted
to you, you are allowed to have it.

・ **pose** [pouz] v. 자세를 취하다; (위협·문제 등을) 제기하다; n. 포즈, 자세
If you pose for a photograph or painting, you stay in a particular position
so that someone can photograph you or paint you.

‡ **sign** [sain] v. 서명하다; 신호를 보내다; n. 표지판, 간판; 징후; 몸짓
When you sign a document, you write your name on it, usually at the
end or in a special space.

‡ **dozen** [dʌzn] n. (pl.) 다수, 여러 개; 12개; 십여 개
If you refer to dozens of things or people, you are emphasizing that there
are very many of them.

autograph [ɔ́ːtougræf] n. (유명인의) 사인; v. 사인을 해주다
An autograph is the signature of someone famous which is specially
written for a fan to keep.

recognize [rékəgnàiz] v. 알아보다; 인식하다; 공인하다
If you recognize someone or something, you know who that person is or what that thing is.

occupy [ákjupài] v. (방·주택·건물을) 사용하다; (공간·지역·시간을) 차지하다; 점령하다
If a room or something such as a seat is occupied, someone is using it, so that it is not available for anyone else.

disappoint [disəpɔ́int] v. 실망시키다, 실망을 안겨 주다; 좌절시키다
(disappointment n. 실망, 낙심)
Disappointment is the feeling of being unhappy because something has not happened or been as good as you expected or hoped.

lessen [lesn] v. (크기·강도 등이) 줄다
If something lessens or you lessen it, it becomes smaller in size, amount, degree, or importance.

crowd [kraud] n. 사람들, 군중; v. 가득 메우다; (생각이 마음속에) 밀려오다
A crowd is a large group of people who have come together.

gather [gǽðər] v. (사람들이) 모이다; (여기저기 있는 것을) 모으다
If people gather somewhere or if someone gathers people somewhere, they come together in a group.

demonstrate [démənstrèit] v. (행동으로) 보여주다; 설명하다
If you demonstrate a particular skill, quality, or feeling, you show by your actions that you have it.

stroke [strouk] n. (공을 치는) 타격, 스트로크; 치기, 때리기; v. 쓰다듬다, 어루만지다
In sports such as tennis, baseball, cricket, and golf, a stroke is the action of hitting the ball.

be known for idiom ~로 알려져 있다
If someone or something is known for a particular achievement or feature, they are familiar to many people because of that achievement or feature.

terrible [térəbl] a. 형편없는; 끔찍한, 소름끼치는; (나쁜 정도가) 극심한
If something is terrible, it is very bad or of very poor quality.

: temper [témpər] n. (걸핏하면 화를 내는) 성질; v. 누그러뜨리다, 완화시키다

If you refer to someone's temper or say that they have a temper, you mean that they become angry very easily.

. squeeze [skwiːz] v. (좁은 곳에) 비집고 들어가다; (꼭) 짜다; n. (손으로 꼭) 쥐기

If you squeeze a person or thing somewhere or if they squeeze there, they manage to get through or into a small space.

복습 cover [kávər] v. 취재하다; 덮다; 씌우다; n. 덮개; 몸을 숨길 곳

If journalists, newspapers, or television companies cover an event, they report on it.

. thrill [θril] n. 흥분, 설렘; 전율; v. 열광시키다, 정말 신나게 하다

If something gives you a thrill, it gives you a sudden feeling of great excitement, pleasure, or fear.

: tiny [táini] a. 아주 작은

Something or someone that is tiny is extremely small.

. sneeze [sniːz] n. 재채기; v. 재채기하다

When you sneeze, you suddenly take in your breath and then blow it down your nose noisily without being able to stop yourself, for example because you have a cold.

. glare [glɛər] v. 노려보다; 환하다, 눈부시다; n. 노려봄; 환한 빛, 눈부심

If you glare at someone, you look at them with an angry expression on your face.

granny [grǽni] n. 할머니

Some people refer to their grandmother as granny.

: burst [bəːrst] v. (burst–burst) 터지다, 파열하다; 불쑥 움직이다; n. (갑자기) 한바탕 ~을 함
(burst into idiom (갑자기) ~을 터뜨리다)

If you burst into something, you suddenly start doing it.

: mean [miːn] a. 못된, 심술궂은; v. 의미하다

If someone is being mean, they are being unkind to another person, for example by not allowing them to do something.

‡ **fellow** [félou] n. 녀석, 친구; 동료; a. 동료의
A fellow is a man or boy.

⋆ **whisper** [hwíspər] v. 속삭이다, 소곤거리다; 은밀히 말하다; n. 속삭임, 소곤거리는 소리
When you whisper, you say something very quietly, using your breath
rather than your throat, so that only one person can hear you.

‡ **stand** [stænd] v. 참다, 견디다; 서 있다; n. 가판대, 좌판; (경기장의) 관중석
If you cannot stand someone or something, you dislike them very
strongly.

hold it idiom 잠깐 기다려!
You can use 'hold it' in order to tell someone to wait a moment.

⋆ **director** [diréktər] n. (영화·연극의) 감독; (회사의) 임원
The director of a play, film, or television program is the person who
decides how it will appear on stage or screen, and who tells the actors
and technical staff what to do.

‡ **spot** [spat] v. 발견하다, 찾다, 알아채다; n. (작은) 점; (특정한) 곳
If you spot something or someone, you notice them.

‡ **break** [breik] n. 운수; (작업 중의) 휴식; v. 깨다, 부수다
A break is a lucky opportunity that someone gets to achieve something.

⋆ **impress** [imprés] v. 깊은 인상을 주다, 감동을 주다 (impressed a. 감명을 받은)
If something impresses you, you feel great admiration for it.

‡ **swing** [swiŋ] v. 방향을 바꾸다; (전후·좌우로) 흔들다; 휙 움직이다; n. 흔들기; 휘두르기
If something swings in a particular direction or if you swing it in that
direction, it moves in that direction with a smooth, curving movement.

복습 **pajamas** [pədʒáːməz] n. (바지와 상의로 된) 잠옷
A pair of pajamas consists of loose trousers and a loose jacket that
people, especially men, wear in bed.

‡ **personal** [pɔ́rsənl] a. 개인적인; 개인의
A personal opinion, quality, or thing belongs or relates to one particular
person rather than to other people.

* **delightful** [diláitfəl] a. 정말 기분 좋은, 마음에 드는
If you describe something or someone as delightful, you mean they are very pleasant.

cheer [tʃiər] v. 환호하다; 응원하다; n. 쾌활함, 생기; 환호
When people cheer, they shout loudly to show their approval or to encourage someone who is doing something such as taking part in a game.

wave [weiv] v. (손·팔을) 흔들다; 흔들리다; n. 파도, 물결; (손·팔을) 흔들기
If you wave or wave your hand, you move your hand from side to side in the air, usually in order to say hello or goodbye to someone.

blow a kiss idiom ~에게 (손시늉으로) 키스를 보내다
If you blow someone a kiss or blow a kiss, you touch the palm of your hand lightly with your lips, and then blow across your hand toward the person, in order to show them your affection.

jealous [dʒéləs] a. 질투하는; 시샘하는
If you are jealous of another person's possessions or qualities, you feel angry or bitter because you do not have them.

attention [əténʃən] n. 관심, 흥미; 주의 (집중), 주목
Attention is great interest that is shown in someone or something, particularly by the general public.

whack [wæk] v. 세게 치다, 후려치다; (되는대로) 툭 던지다; n. 퍽, 철썩; 강타
If you whack someone or something, you hit them hard.

fence [fens] n. 울타리; 장애물; v. 울타리를 치다
A fence is a barrier between two areas of land, made of wood or wire supported by posts.

notice [nóutis] v. 알아채다, 인지하다; 주의하다; n. 신경씀, 주목, 알아챔
If you notice something or someone, you become aware of them.

* **champion** [tʃǽmpiən] n. 챔피언, 대회 우승자
A champion is someone who has won the first prize in a competition, contest, or fight.

growl [graul] v. 으르렁거리듯 말하다; 으르렁거리다; n. 으르렁거리는 소리
If someone growls something, they say something in a low, rough, and angry voice.

go on idiom 말을 계속하다; (어떤 상황이) 계속되다
To go on means to continue speaking after a short pause.

volunteer [vàləntíər] n. 자원하는 사람; 자원 봉사자; v. 자원하다; 제안하다
A volunteer is someone who offers to do a particular task or job without being forced to do it.

compare [kəmpéər] v. 필적하다, 비교가 되다; 비교하다
If you compare one person or thing to another, you say that they are like the other person or thing.

signal [sígnəl] v. (동작·소리로) 신호를 보내다; 암시하다; n. 신호; 징조
If you signal to someone, you make a gesture or sound in order to send them a particular message.

serve [səːrv] n. (테니스 등에서) 서브; v. (음식을) 제공하다; (상품·서비스를) 제공하다
A serve is a hit of a ball that starts the play in a game such as tennis.

grip [grip] n. 잡는 방식; 꽉 붙잡음; 통제; v. 꽉 잡다; (마음·흥미·시선을) 끌다
A grip is a firm, strong hold on something.

net [net] n. (테니스) 네트; 그물, 망; v. 그물로 잡다; (무엇을) 획득하다
In games such as tennis, the net is the piece of netting across the center of the court which the ball has to go over.

entire [intáiər] a. 전체의, 온 (entirely ad. 완전히, 전부)
Entirely means completely and not just partly.

knock [nak] v. 치다, 부딪치다; (문 등을) 두드리다; n. 문 두드리는 소리; 부딪침
If you knock something, you touch or hit it roughly, especially so that it falls or moves.

whiz [hwiz] v. 쌩 하고 지나가다; 잽싸게 하다; n. 윙, 핑 (하는 소리)
If something whizzes somewhere, it moves there very fast.

: angle [ǽŋgl] n. 각도, 각; v. 비스듬히 움직이다
An angle is the difference in direction between two lines or surfaces.
Angles are measured in degrees.

복습 foolish [fúːliʃ] a. 바보 같은 (기분이 들게 하는); 어리석은
If you look or feel foolish, you look or feel so silly or ridiculous that people
are likely to laugh at you.

race [reis] v. 쏜살같이 가다; 경주하다; n. 경주; 경쟁; 인종, 종족
If you race somewhere, you go there as quickly as possible.

back and forth idiom 여기저기에, 왔다갔다; 앞뒤로; 좌우로
If someone moves back and forth, they repeatedly move in one direction
and then in the opposite direction.

: practical [prǽktikəl] a. 거의 완전한, 사실상의; 현실적인; 타당한
(practically ad. 사실상, 거의)
Practically means almost, but not completely or exactly.

: shot [ʃɑt] n. (한 번) 치기; 시도; 발사; 사진
In sports such as football, golf, or tennis, a shot is an act of kicking,
hitting, or throwing the ball, especially in an attempt to score a point.

skid [skid] v. 미끄러지다; n. (차량의) 미끄러짐
If a vehicle skids, it slides sideways or forward while moving, for example
when you are trying to stop it suddenly on a wet road.

• halt [hɔːlt] n. 멈춤, 중단; v. 멈추다, 서다; 중단시키다
If someone or something comes to a halt, they stop moving.

• bang [bæŋ] v. 쿵 하고 찧다; 쾅 하고 치다; 쾅 하고 닫다; n. 쾅 (하는 소리)
If you bang a part of your body, you accidentally knock it against
something and hurt yourself.

복습 knee [niː] n. 무릎; v. 무릎으로 치다
Your knee is the place where your leg bends.

^복^습 nasty [næsti] a. 못된, 심술궂은; 끔찍한, 형편없는

If you describe a person or their behavior as nasty, you mean that they behave in an unkind and unpleasant way.

* slash [slæʃ] v. 긋다, 베다; 대폭 줄이다; n. (칼 등으로) 긋기

If you slash at a person or thing, you quickly hit at them with something such as a knife.

∶ bullet [búlit] n. 총알

A bullet is a small piece of metal with a pointed or rounded end, which is fired out of a gun.

∶ shame [ʃeim] n. 수치(심), 창피; 애석한 일; v. 창피스럽게 하다; 망신시키다

You can use shame in expressions such as shame on you and shame on him to indicate that someone ought to feel shame for something they have said or done.

* fist [fist] n. 주먹

Your hand is referred to as your fist when you have bent your fingers in toward the palm in order to hit someone, to make an angry gesture, or to hold something.

* bet [bet] v. (~이) 틀림없다; (내기 등에) 돈을 걸다; n. 내기; 짐작, 추측

You use expressions such as 'I bet,' 'I'll bet,' and 'you can bet' to indicate that you are sure something is true.

* bounce [bauns] v. (공 등이) 튀다, 뛰어오르다; 깡충깡충 뛰다; n. (공 등이) 튐; 탄력

When an object such as a ball bounces or when you bounce it, it moves upward from a surface or away from it immediately after hitting it.

* rally [ræli] v. 공을 서로 받아치다; 결집하다; n. (대규모) 집회

In sports such as tennis, to rally means to exchange strokes before a point is won.

* glide [glaid] v. 미끄러지듯 움직이다; 활공하다; n. 미끄러지는 듯한 움직임

If you glide somewhere, you move silently and in a smooth and effortless way.

swift [swift] a. 빠른, 날랜; 신속한, 재빠른 (swiftly ad. 신속히, 빨리)
Something that is swift moves very quickly.

lob [lab] v. (공을 높이) 치다; (공중으로 높이) 던지다
If you lob something, you throw it so that it goes quite high in the air.

yell [jel] v. 고함치다, 소리 지르다; n. 고함, 외침
If you yell, you shout loudly, usually because you are excited, angry, or in pain.

besides [bisáidz] ad. 게다가, 뿐만 아니라; 또(한)
Besides is used to emphasize an additional point that you are making, especially one that you consider to be important.

tremendous [triméndəs] a. 엄청난; 굉장한, 대단한
You use tremendous to emphasize how strong a feeling or quality is, or how large an amount is.

modest [mádist] a. 겸손한; 신중한; 적당한 (modestly ad. 겸손하게, 조심성 있게)
If you say that someone is modest, you approve of them because they do not talk much about their abilities or achievements.

friendly [fréndli] a. (행동이) 친절한, 우호적인; 상냥한, 다정한
If someone is friendly, they behave in a pleasant, kind way, and like to be with other people.

frankly [frǽŋkli] ad. 솔직히, 솔직히 말하면
You use frankly when you are expressing an opinion or feeling to emphasize that you mean what you are saying, especially when the person you are speaking to may not like it.

warm up idiom 몸을 천천히 풀다, 준비 운동을 하다
If you warm up for something such as exercise or performance, you do gentle exercise or practice to prepare for it.

reporter [ripɔ́:rtər] n. (보도) 기자, 리포터
A reporter is someone who writes news articles or who broadcasts news reports.

weigh [wei] v. 무게가 ~이다; 무게를 달다
If someone or something weighs a particular amount, this amount is how heavy they are.

none of your business idiom 상관 마, 참견 마
If you say to someone 'it's none of your business,' you are rudely telling them not to ask about something that does not concern them.

celebrated [séləbrèitid] a. 유명한
A celebrated person or thing is famous and much admired.

newscaster [njúːzkæstər] n. (라디오·텔레비전의) 뉴스 프로 진행자
A newscaster is a person who reads the news on the radio or on television.

close-up [klóus-ʌp] n. 근접 촬영(한 사진), 클로즈업
A close-up is a photograph or a picture in a film that shows a lot of detail because it is taken very near to the subject.

interrupt [intərʌ́pt] v. (말·행동을) 방해하다; 중단시키다; 차단하다
If someone or something interrupts a process or activity, they stop it for a period of time.

bother [báðər] v. 신경 쓰이게 하다; 귀찮게 하다; 신경 쓰다, 애를 쓰다; n. 성가심
If something bothers you, or if you bother about it, it worries, annoys, or upsets you.

jar [dʒaːr] n. 병; 단지; v. 불쾌감을 주다, (신경을) 거슬리다
A jar is a glass container with a lid that is used for storing food.

rubber [rʌ́bər] a. 고무의; n. 고무
Rubber is a strong, waterproof, elastic substance, which is used for making tires, boots, and other products.

The Brothers Fly

1. What did Stanley wish for Arthur?

   A. He wished for Arthur to be the strongest man in the world.

   B. He wished for Arthur to be the bravest superhero in the world.

   C. He wished for Arthur to be the fastest flier in the world.

   D. He wished for Arthur to be the smartest president in the world.

2. How could Stanley and Arthur fly?

   A. By telling Prince Haraz where they wanted to go

   B. By holding their breath

   C. By thinking of flying

   D. By flapping their arms

3. How did the airplane pilots react when they saw the brothers and genie flying?
   A. They were excited to see people flying.
   B. They thought they were just imagining it all.
   C. They felt annoyed that the brothers and genie were flying so close to the plane.
   D. They were worried that the brothers and genie would get hurt.

4. What was happening on the ship?
   A. Robbers were stealing a helicopter.
   B. Robbers were taking things from passengers.
   C. The captain and officers were fighting robbers.
   D. The passengers were having a big party.

5. How did Arthur stop the robbers?
   A. He pushed their helicopter back down onto the ship deck.
   B. He broke the engine of their helicopter.
   C. He picked them up and took them away from the ship.
   D. He tied them up with rope.

Check Your Reading Speed
1분에 몇 단어를 읽는지 리딩 속도를 측정해보세요.

$$\frac{1,692 \text{ words}}{\text{reading time (\quad) sec}} \times 60 = (\quad) \text{ WPM}$$

Build Your Vocabulary

: complain [kəmpléin] v. 불평하다, 항의하다
If you complain about a situation, you say that you are not satisfied with it.

president [prézədənt] n. 대통령; 회장
The president of a country that has no king or queen is the person who is the head of state of that country.

mighty [máiti] a. 강력한, 힘센; ad. 대단히, 굉장히
Mighty is used to describe something that is very large or powerful.

pajamas [pədʒáːməz] n. (바지와 상의로 된) 잠옷
A pair of pajamas consists of loose trousers and a loose jacket that people, especially men, wear in bed.

rub [rʌb] v. (손·손수건 등을 대고) 문지르다; (두 손 등을) 맞비비다; n. 문지르기, 비비기
If you rub an object or a surface, you move a cloth backward and forward over it in order to clean or dry it.

grant [grænt] v. 승인하다, 허락하다; 인정하다; n. 보조금
If someone in authority grants you something, or if something is granted to you, you are allowed to have it.

disappoint [dìsəpɔ́int] v. 실망시키다, 실망을 안겨 주다; 좌절시키다
(disappointed a. 실망한, 낙담한)
If you are disappointed, you are rather sad because something has not happened or because something is not as good as you had hoped.

punch [pʌntʃ] v. 주먹으로 치다; 구멍을 뚫다; n. 주먹으로 한 대 침

If you punch someone or something, you hit them hard with your fist.

fist [fist] n. 주먹

Your hand is referred to as your fist when you have bent your fingers in toward the palm in order to hit someone, to make an angry gesture, or to hold something.

flap [flæp] v. 펄럭거리다; (새가 날개를) 퍼덕거리다; n. 퍼덕거림; 덮개

If you flap your arms, you move them quickly up and down as if they were the wings of a bird.

relieve [rili:v] v. (불쾌감·고통 등을) 없애 주다; 안도하게 하다; 완화하다

If something relieves an unpleasant feeling or situation, it makes it less unpleasant or causes it to disappear completely.

drawer [drɔ:r] n. 서랍

A drawer is part of a desk, chest, or other piece of furniture that is shaped like a box and is designed for putting things in.

marble [ma:rbl] n. (아이들이 가지고 노는) 구슬; 대리석

A marble is a small ball, usually made of colored or transparent glass, that is used in children's games.

clip [klip] n. 클립, 종이 집게; (짧게) 깎음; v. 클립으로 고정하다; 깎다, 자르다

A clip is a small device, usually made of metal or plastic, that is specially shaped for holding things together.

ridiculous [ridíkjuləs] a. 웃기는, 말도 안 되는, 터무니없는

If you say that something or someone is ridiculous, you mean that they are very foolish.

tidy [táidi] v. 치우다, 정돈하다; a. 단정한, 말쑥한, 깔끔한

When you tidy a place such as a room or cupboard, you make it neat by putting things in their proper places.

adventure [ædvéntʃər] n. 모험; 모험심

If someone has an adventure, they become involved in an unusual, exciting, and rather dangerous journey or series of events.

bedtime [bédtàim] n. 취침 시간, 잠자리에 드는 시간
Your bedtime is the time when you usually go to bed.

hold one's breath idiom (흥분·공포 등으로) 숨을 죽이다
If you say that someone is holding their breath, you mean that they are waiting anxiously or excitedly for something to happen.

expect [ikspékt] v. 예상하다, 기대하다
If you expect something to happen, you believe that it will happen.

sweep [swiːp] v. (swept–swept) 휩쓸고 가다; (빗자루로) 쓸다; n. 쓸기, 비질하기
If you are swept somewhere, you are taken there very quickly.

elbow [élbou] n. 팔꿈치; v. (팔꿈치로) 밀치다
Your elbow is the part of your arm where the upper and lower halves of the arm are joined.

visible [vízəbl] a. (눈에) 보이는, 알아볼 수 있는; 뚜렷한 (invisible a. 보이지 않는)
If you describe something as invisible, you mean that it cannot be seen, for example because it is transparent, hidden, or very small.

glide [glaid] v. 활공하다; 미끄러지듯 움직이다; n. 미끄러지는 듯한 움직임
When birds or airplanes glide, they float on air currents.

toe [tou] n. 발가락
Your toes are the five movable parts at the end of each foot.

heads up idiom 조심해라!
Yoy use 'heads up!' to warn someone about something dangerous or call for their attention.

lean [liːn] v. 기울이다, (몸을) 숙이다; ～에 기대다; a. 호리호리한
When you lean in a particular direction, you bend your body in that direction.

breeze [briːz] n. 산들바람, 미풍; 식은 죽 먹기; v. 경쾌하게 움직이다
A breeze is a gentle wind.

extra [ékstrə] a. 여분의, 추가의; n. 추가되는 것; ad. 각별히, 특별히

You use extra to describe an amount, person, or thing that is added to others of the same kind, or that can be added to others of the same kind.

robe [roub] n. 가운; 예복, 대례복 (bathrobe n. 목욕용 가운)

A bathrobe is a loose piece of clothing made of the same material as towels. You wear it before or after you have a bath or a swim.

glove [glʌv] n. 장갑; v. 장갑을 끼다

Gloves are pieces of clothing which cover your hands and wrists and have individual sections for each finger.

float [flout] v. (물 위나 공중에서) 떠가다; (물에) 뜨다; n. 부표

Something that floats in or through the air hangs in it or moves slowly and gently through it.

level off idiom 수평 비행을 하다

If a airplane levels off, it becomes level or horizontal after rising or falling.

speed [spi:d] v. 빨리 가다; 더 빠르게 하다; n. 속도

If you speed somewhere, you move or travel there quickly, usually in a vehicle.

steady [stédi] a. 꾸준한; 흔들림 없는, 안정된; v. 흔들리지 않다, 진정되다
(steadily ad. 꾸준히)

A steady situation continues or develops gradually without any interruptions and is not likely to change quickly.

side by side idiom 나란히

If two people or things are side by side, they are next to each other.

gain [gein] v. (경험 등을) 쌓다; 얻다; n. 증가; 이득

If a person or place gains something such as an ability or quality, they gradually get more of it.

confident [kánfədənt] a. 자신감 있는; 확신하는 (confidence n. 자신(감); 확신)

If you have confidence, you feel sure about your abilities, qualities, or ideas.

keep an eye on idiom ~을 계속 지켜보다
If you keep an eye on someone or something, you watch or check them to make sure that they are safe.

twinkle [twiŋkl] v. 반짝반짝 빛나다; (눈이) 반짝거리다; n. 반짝거림
If a star or a light twinkles, it shines with an unsteady light which rapidly and constantly changes from bright to faint.

orchestra [ɔ́:rkəstrə] n. 오케스트라, 관현악단
An orchestra is a large group of musicians who play a variety of different instruments together.

tone [toun] n. 음조, 음색; 어조
The tone of a sound is its particular quality.

note [nout] n. 음(표); 메모; 편지, 쪽지; v. ~에 주목하다
In music, a note is the sound of a particular pitch, or a written symbol representing this sound.

join hands idiom (~와) 손을 잡다
If two people join hands, they hold each other's hands.

circle [sə́:rkl] v. 빙빙 돌다; 에워싸다, 둘러싸다; n. 원형
If an aircraft or a bird circles or circles something, it moves round in a circle in the air.

blaze [bleiz] n. 휘황찬란한 빛; 불길; v. 눈부시게 빛나다; 활활 타다
A blaze is a strong bright light or area of color.

rink [riŋk] n. (= ice rink) 아이스 링크
A rink is a large area covered with ice where people go to iceskate.

distance [dístəns] n. 먼 곳; 거리; v. (~에) 관여하지 않다
(in the distance idiom 저 멀리)
If you can see something in the distance, you can see it, far away from you.

blink [bliŋk] v. (불빛이) 깜박거리다; 눈을 깜박이다; n. 눈을 깜박거림
When a light blinks, it flashes on and off.

: chase [ʧeis] v. 뒤쫓다, 추적하다; 추구하다; n. 추적, 추격; 추구함
If you chase someone, or chase after them, you run after them or follow them quickly in order to catch or reach them.

catch up idiom 따라잡다, 따라가다
If you catch up with someone or something, you reach them ahead of you by going faster than them.

whoosh [hwuːʃ] n. 쉭 하는 소리; v. (아주 빠르게) 휙 하고 지나가다
People sometimes say 'whoosh' when they are emphasizing the fact that something happens very suddenly or very fast.

: flash [flæʃ] v. 휙 움직이다; (잠깐) 번쩍이다; (눈 등이) 번득이다; n. 번쩍임; 순간
If something flashes past or by, it moves past you so fast that you cannot see it properly.

: sail [seil] n. 돛; v. 항해하다; 미끄러지듯 나아가다
Sails are large pieces of material attached to the mast of a ship. The wind blows against the sails and pushes the ship along.

passenger [pǽsəndʒər] n. 승객
A passenger in a vehicle such as a bus, boat, or plane is a person who is travelling in it, but who is not driving it or working on it.

tiny [táini] a. 아주 작은
Something or someone that is tiny is extremely small.

. tray [trei] n. 쟁반; (납작한 플라스틱) 상자
A tray is a flat piece of wood, plastic, or metal, which usually has raised edges and which is used for carrying things, especially food and drinks.

. comic [kámik] n. (= comic book) 만화책, 만화잡지;
a. 웃기는, 재미있는; 코미디의, 희극의
A comic is a magazine that contains stories told in pictures.

zoom [zuːm] v. 쌩 하고 가다; 급등하다; n. (빠르게) 쌩 하고 지나가는 소리
If you zoom somewhere, you go there very quickly.

: stretch [stretʃ] v. (팔·다리를) 뻗다; (길이·폭 등을) 늘이다; n. (길게) 뻗은 지역
When you stretch, you put your arms or legs out straight and tighten your muscles.

복습 mean [miːn] a. 못된, 심술궂은; v. 의미하다
If someone is being mean, they are being unkind to another person, for example by not allowing them to do something.

stick out idiom (툭) 튀어나오다, ~을 내밀다
If something is sticking out from a surface or object, it extends up or away from it.

: tongue [tʌŋ] n. 혀; 말버릇
Your tongue is the soft movable part inside your mouth which you use for tasting, eating, and speaking.

scowl [skaul] v. 노려보다, 쏘아보다; n. 노려봄, 쏘아봄
When someone scowls, an angry or hostile expression appears on their face.

⋆ lap [læp] n. 무릎; (경주에서 트랙의) 한 바퀴
If you have something on your lap when you are sitting down, it is on top of your legs and near to your body.

복습 puff [pʌf] v. 부풀어오르다; (많은 양의 연기·김을) 내뿜다;
n. 훅 (부는 소리); (공기·연기 등의) 작은 양
If something puffs up or you puff it up, it swells or you make it swell and increase in size.

⋆ wrinkle [riŋkl] v. 찡그리다; 주름이 지다; n. 주름
When you wrinkle your nose or forehead, or when it wrinkles, you tighten the muscles in your face so that the skin folds.

: thumb [θʌm] n. 엄지손가락; v. 엄지손가락으로 건드리다
Your thumb is the short thick part on the side of your hand next to your four fingers.

wriggle [rigl] v. (몸을) 꿈틀거리다; 꿈틀거리며 가다; n. 꿈틀거리기
If you wriggle or wriggle part of your body, you twist and turn with quick movements, for example because you are uncomfortable.

cockpit [kákpit] n. (항공기·경주용 자동차의) 조종석
In an airplane or racing car, the cockpit is the part where the pilot or driver sits.

pilot [páilət] n. 조종사, 비행사
A pilot is a person who is trained to fly an aircraft.

hover [hʌ́vər] v. (허공을) 맴돌다; 서성이다; 주저하다; n. 공중을 떠다님
To hover means to stay in the same position in the air without moving forward or backward.

tip [tip] n. (뾰족한) 끝; v. 기울이다, 젖히다; 살짝 건드리다
The tip of something long and narrow is the end of it.

joke [dʒouk] v. 농담하다; 농담 삼아 말하다; n. 농담; 웃음거리
(joker n. 농담을 잘하는 사람)
Someone who is a joker likes making jokes or doing amusing things.

stare [stɛər] v. 빤히 쳐다보다, 응시하다; n. 빤히 쳐다보기, 응시
If you stare at someone or something, you look at them for a long time.

mention [ménʃən] v. 말하다, 언급하다; n. 언급, 거론
If you mention something, you say something about it, usually briefly.

definite [défənit] a. 확실한, 확고한; 분명한, 뚜렷한 (definitely ad. 그렇고말고)
You use definitely to emphasize that something is the case, or to emphasize the strength of your intention or opinion.

ablaze [əbléiz] a. 불타는 듯한, 환한; 불길에 휩싸인
If a place is ablaze with lights or colors, it is very bright because of them.

make one's way idiom 나아가다, 가다
When you make your way somewhere, you walk or travel there.

whiz [hwiz] v. 쌩 하고 지나가다; 잽싸게 하다; n. 윙, 핑 (하는 소리)
If something whizzes somewhere, it moves there very fast.

marvel [máːrvəl] v. 경이로워하다, 경탄하다; n. 경이(로운 사람·것)
If you marvel at something, you express your great surprise, wonder, or admiration.

enormous [inɔ́ːrməs] a. 막대한, 거대한
Something that is enormous is extremely large in size or amount.

deck [dek] n. (배의) 갑판; 층; v. 꾸미다, 장식하다
A deck on a vehicle such as a bus or ship is a lower or upper area of it.

layer [léiər] n. 층, 막; v. 층층이 놓다
A layer of a material or substance is a quantity or piece of it that covers a surface or that is between two other things.

sparkle [spaːrkl] v. 반짝이다; 생기 넘치다; n. 반짝거림, 광채
If something sparkles, it is clear and bright and shines with a lot of very small points of light.

rob [rab] v. (사람·장소를) 도둑질하다 (robbery n. 강도 사건)
Robbery is the crime of stealing money or property from a bank, shop, or vehicle, often by using force or threats.

crowd [kraud] v. 가득 메우다; (생각이 마음속에) 밀려오다; n. 사람들, 군중
If a group of people crowd a place, there are so many of them there that it is full.

line up idiom ~을 한 줄로 세우다
If you line people or things up, you arrange them in a line or a row.

jewelry [dʒúːəlri] n. 보석류, 장신구
Jewelry is ornaments that people wear, for example rings, bracelets, and necklaces. It is often made of a valuable metal such as gold, and sometimes decorated with precious stones.

captain [kǽptən] n. 선장, 함장; [군사] 대위, 대령; v. 주장이 되다
The captain of a ship is the sailor in charge of it.

: bridge [bridʒ] n. [항해] 선교, 함교; 다리; v. 다리를 놓다
The bridge is the place on a ship from which it is steered.

복습 fellow [félou] a. 동료의; n. 녀석, 친구; 동료
You use fellow to describe people who are in the same situation as you, or people you feel you have something in common with.

. officer [ɔ́ːfisər] n. 운항 승무원; 장교; 경찰관
A officer is a person licensed to take full or partial responsibility for the operation of a ship.

: struggle [strʌgl] v. 몸부림치다, 허우적거리다; 힘겹게 나아가다; n. 투쟁, 분투; 몸부림
If you struggle to move yourself or to move a heavy object, you try to do it, but it is difficult.

: chain [tʃéin] v. 사슬로 매다; n. 쇠사슬; 연쇄, 일련
If a person or thing is chained to something, they are fastened to it with a chain.

railing [réiliŋ] n. 난간; 울타리
A fence made from metal bars is called a railing or railings.

crook [kruk] n. 도둑, 사기꾼; v. (손가락이나 팔을) 구부리다
A crook is a dishonest person or a criminal.

복습 stuff [stʌf] n. 것, 물건; v. 채워 넣다; 쑤셔 넣다
You can use stuff to refer to things such as a substance, a collection of things, events, or ideas, or the contents of something in a general way without mentioning the thing itself by name.

: strength [streŋθ] n. 힘, 기운; 강도
Your strength is the physical energy that you have, which gives you the ability to perform various actions, such as lifting or moving things.

: tear [tɛər] ① v. (tore-torn) 뜯어 내다; 찢다, 뜯다; n. 찢어진 곳, 구멍 ② n. 눈물
If you tear something away, you pull it violently from the thing it is attached to.

bind [baind] v. (bound-bound) 묶다; 결속시키다; 굳다, 뭉치다
If you bind something or someone, you tie rope, string, tape, or other material around them so that they are held firmly.

amaze [əméiz] v. (대단히) 놀라게 하다; 경악하게 하다 (amazed a. (대단히) 놀란)
If something amazes you, it surprises you very much.

stumble [stʌmbl] v. 발을 헛디디다; (말·글 읽기를 하다가) 더듬거리다
If you stumble, you put your foot down awkwardly while you are walking or running and nearly fall over.

drop [drap] v. 떨어뜨리다; 약해지다; 낮추다; n. 방울; 소량, 조금
If you drop something, you accidentally let it fall.

lordy [lɔ́ːrdi] int. 저런, 어머
People sometimes say 'lordy' as an exclamation of surprise or dismay.

yell [jel] v. 고함치다, 소리 지르다; n. 고함, 외침
If you yell, you shout loudly, usually because you are excited, angry, or in pain.

resist [rizíst] v. 참다, 견디다; 저항하다; 굴하지 않다
If you resist doing something, or resist the temptation to do it, you stop yourself from doing it although you would like to do it.

show off idiom ~을 자랑하다; 돋보이게 하다
To show off means to try to impress other people with your abilities, wealth, or intelligence.

fierce [fiərs] a. 사나운, 험악한; 격렬한, 맹렬한
A fierce animal or person is very aggressive or angry.

crime [kraim] n. 범죄; 죄악
A crime is an illegal action or activity for which a person can be punished by law.

exclaim [ikskléim] v. 소리치다, 외치다 (exclamation n. 감탄사)
An exclamation is a sound, word, or sentence that is spoken suddenly or loudly and that expresses excitement, admiration, shock, or anger.

swoop [swuːp] v. 급강하하다, 위에서 덮치다; 급습하다; n. 급강하; 급습
When a bird or airplane swoops, it suddenly moves downward through the air in a smooth curving movement.

: **tie** [tai] v. (매듭을 지어) 묶다; 구속하다; n. 끈; (강한) 유대 (untie v. (매듭 등을) 풀다)
If you untie something such as string or rope, you undo it so that there is no knot or so that it is no longer tying something.

flare [flɛər] v. 아랫부분 쪽으로 폭이 넓어지다; 확 타오르다; n. 확 타오르는 불길
If something such as a dress flares, it spreads outward at one end to form a wide shape.

⋅ **cape** [keip] n. 어깨 망토
A cape is a short cloak.

⋅ **defend** [difénd] v. 방어하다, 수비하다; 옹호하다, 변호하다 (defender n. 수호자)
If you defend someone or something, you take action in order to protect them.

⋅ **innocent** [ínəsənt] a. 무고한; 무죄인, 결백한; 순진한
Innocent people are those who are not involved in a crime or conflict, but are injured or killed as a result of it.

: **frighten** [fraitn] v. 겁먹게 하다, 놀라게 하다 (frightened a. 겁먹은, 무서워하는)
If you are frightened, you are anxious or afraid, often because of something that has just happened or that you think may happen.

⋅ **grab** [græb] v. (와락·단단히) 붙잡다; 급히 ~하다; n. 와락 잡아채려고 함
If you grab something, you take it or pick it up suddenly and roughly.

복습 **set out** idiom (여행을) 시작하다; ~을 진열하다
If you set out, you leave a place and begin a journey, especially a long journey.

복습 **cheer** [tʃiər] n. 환호; 쾌활함, 생기; v. 환호하다; 응원하다
A cheer is a shout of encouragement, praise, or joy.

: grateful [gréitfəl] a. 고마워하는, 감사하는

If you are grateful for something that someone has given you or done for you, you have warm, friendly feelings toward them and wish to thank them.

· crew [kru:] n. 승무원; 무리, 일당

The crew of a ship, an aircraft, or a spacecraft is the people who work on and operate it.

hooray [huréi] int. 만세

People sometimes shout 'hooray!' when they are very happy and excited about something.

· rescue [réskju:] v. 구하다, 구출하다; n. 구출, 구조, 구제 (rescuer n. 구조자, 구출자)

If you rescue someone, you get them out of a dangerous or unpleasant situation.

· outline [áutlàin] n. 윤곽; v. 윤곽을 보여주다

The outline of something is its general shape, especially when it cannot be clearly seen.

whisper [hwíspər] n. 속삭임, 소곤거리는 소리; v. 속삭이다, 소곤거리다; 은밀히 말하다

A whisper is a very quiet way of saying something so that other people cannot hear you.

rush [rʌʃ] v. 급히 움직이다; 서두르다; 재촉하다; n. 혼잡, 분주함

If air or liquid rushes somewhere, it flows there suddenly and quickly.

· tiring [táiəriŋ] a. 피곤하게 만드는, 피곤한

If you describe something as tiring, you mean that it makes you tired so that you want to rest or sleep.

sight [sait] n. 시야; 광경, 모습; 보기, 봄; v. 갑자기 보다

(come into sight idiom 보이기 시작하다)

If someone or something comes into sight, they become visible.

The Last Wish

1. **What was one unexpected consequence of the wishes that had come true?**

   A. Tom McRude had become even meaner.

   B. Mrs. Lambchop no longer had any privacy.

   C. Mr. Lambchop no longer had the ability to play tennis.

   D. Arthur had become too popular.

2. **Why did Mrs. Lambchop make hot chocolate for everyone?**

   A. She figured that it would help everyone think.

   B. She wanted to wake everyone up.

   C. She expected that it would make everyone sleepy.

   D. She was hoping to cheer everyone up.

3. What did Mr. Lambchop ask Prince Haraz?

A. He asked if the family could have fifteen more wishes.

B. He asked if the family could keep the Liophant.

C. He asked if Stanley could reverse the wishes he had made.

D. He asked if Stanley could exchange his previous wishes with new ones.

4. What is a training lamp?

A. A lamp that makes wishes permanent

B. A lamp that grants wishes for only fifteen days

C. A lamp that limits the number of wishes that can be granted

D. A lamp that cannot grant wishes to more than one person

5. What was Stanley's last wish?

A. For Prince Haraz to stay with the Lambchops forever

B. For Prince Haraz to be freed from the lamp

C. For Prince Haraz to tell Stanley what he wanted

D. For Prince Haraz to introduce the Lambchops to his genie friends

Check Your Reading Speed
1분에 몇 단어를 읽는지 리딩 속도를 측정해보세요.

$$\frac{1,685 \text{ words}}{\text{reading time (} \quad \text{) sec}} \times 60 = (\quad) \text{ WPM}$$

Build Your Vocabulary

adventure [ædvéntʃər] n. 모험; 모험심 (adventurer n. 모험가)
An adventurer is a person who enjoys going to new, unusual, and exciting places.

anxious [ǽŋkʃəs] a. 불안해하는; 열망하는, 간절히 바라는 (anxiously ad. 걱정스럽게)
If you are anxious, you are nervous or worried about something.

enormous [inɔ́ːrməs] a. 막대한, 거대한
Something that is enormous is extremely large in size or amount.

bowl [boul] n. 한 그릇(의 양); (우묵한) 그릇
The contents of a bowl can be referred to as a bowl of something.

thank goodness idiom (기쁨·안도를 나타내어) 아 고마워라!, 살았다!, 됐다!
You say 'thank goodness,' 'thank God,' or 'thank heavens' when you are very relieved about something.

stern [stəːrn] a. 엄중한, 근엄한; 심각한
Someone who is stern is very serious and strict.

robe [roub] n. 가운; 예복, 대례복
A robe is a piece of clothing, usually made of toweling, which people wear in the house, especially when they have just got up or had a bath.

glove [glʌv] n. 장갑; v. 장갑을 끼다
Gloves are pieces of clothing which cover your hands and wrists and have individual sections for each finger.

74

overheated [òuvərhí:tid] a. 지나치게 더운; (관심·흥분이) 과열된
Someone who is overheated is getting too hot.

go on idiom 말을 계속하다; (어떤 상황이) 계속되다
To go on means to continue speaking after a short pause.

* **tub** [tʌb] n. (= bathtub) 욕조; 통
A tub is the same as a bathtub, which is a long, usually rectangular container which you fill with water and sit in to wash your body.

* **fright** [frait] n. 놀람, 두려움
Fright is a sudden feeling of fear, especially the fear that you feel when something unpleasant surprises you.

apologize [əpálədʒàiz] v. 사과하다
When you apologize to someone, you say that you are sorry that you have hurt them or caused trouble for them.

chase [tʃeis] v. 뒤쫓다, 추적하다; 추구하다; n. 추적, 추격; 추구함
If you chase someone, or chase after them, you run after them or follow them quickly in order to catch or reach them.

rob [rab] v. (사람·장소를) 도둑질하다 (robber n. 강도)
A robber is someone who steals money or property from a bank, a shop, or a vehicle, often by using force or threats.

* **sigh** [sai] n. 한숨; v. 한숨을 쉬다, 한숨짓다; 탄식하듯 말하다
A sigh is a slow breath out that makes a long soft sound, especially because you are disappointed, tired, annoyed, or relaxed.

expect [ikspékt] v. 예상하다, 기대하다 (unexpected a. 예기치 않은, 예상 밖의)
If an event or someone's behavior is unexpected, it surprises you because you did not think that it was likely to happen.

* **consequence** [kánsəkwèns] n. (발생한 일의) 결과; 중요함
The consequences of something are the results or effects of it.

* **exhaust** [igzɔ́ːst] v. 기진맥진하게 하다; 다 써 버리다; n. (자동차 등의) 배기가스
(exhausted a. 기진맥진한)
If something exhausts you, it makes you so tired, either physically or mentally, that you have no energy left.

* **privacy** [práivəsi] n. 사생활; 혼자 있는 상태
If someone or something invades your privacy, they interfere in your life without your permission.

‡ **deserve** [dizɔ́ːrv] v. ~을 당해야 마땅하다; ~을 받을 만하다, ~을 누릴 자격이 있다
If you say that someone got what they deserved, you mean that they deserved the bad thing that happened to them, and you have no sympathy for them.

복습 **shame** [ʃeim] v. 창피스럽게 하다; 망신시키다; n. 수치(심), 창피; 애석한 일
If something shames you, it causes you to feel shame.

복습 **strength** [streŋkθ] n. 힘, 기운; 강도
Your strength is the physical energy that you have, which gives you the ability to perform various actions, such as lifting or moving things.

‡ **criminal** [krímənl] n. 범인, 범죄자; a. 범죄의; 형사상의
A criminal is a person who regularly commits crimes.

복습 **dear** [diər] int. 이런!, 맙소사!; n. 여보, 자기; 얘야; a 사랑하는; ~에게
You can use dear in expressions such as 'oh dear,' 'dear me,' and 'dear, dear' when you are sad, disappointed, or surprised about something.

* **sip** [sip] v. (음료를) 홀짝거리다, 조금씩 마시다; n. 한 모금
If you sip a drink or sip at it, you drink by taking just a small amount at a time.

* **pace** [peis] v. 서성거리다; (일의) 속도를 유지하다; n. 속도; 걸음
If you pace a small area, you keep walking up and down it, because you are anxious or impatient.

복습 **clear one's throat** idiom 목을 가다듬다; 헛기침하다
If you clear your throat, you cough once in order to make it easier to speak or to attract people's attention.

^복^습 attention [əténʃən] n. 주의 (집중), 주목; 관심, 흥미
If you give someone or something your attention, you look at it, listen to it, or think about it carefully.

^복^습 faraway [fɑ́ːrəwei] a. 멀리 떨어진, 먼; 생각이 딴 데 가 있는 듯한
A faraway place is a long distance from you or from a particular place.

^복^습 grateful [gréitfəl] a. 고마워하는, 감사하는
If you are grateful for something that someone has given you or done for you, you have warm, friendly feelings toward them and wish to thank them.

clever [klévər] a. 기발한, 재치 있는; 영리한, 똑똑한
Someone who is clever is intelligent and able to understand things easily or plan things well.

lovable [lʌ́vəbl] a. 사랑스러운, 매력적인
If you describe someone as lovable, you mean that they have attractive qualities, and are easy to like.

afford [əfɔ́ːrd] v. ~할 여유가 있다; 제공하다
If you cannot afford something, you do not have enough money to pay for it.

reverse [rivə́ːrs] v. 뒤집다, 뒤바꾸다; n. (정)반대; a. (정)반대의
When someone or something reverses a decision, policy, or trend, they change it to the opposite decision, policy, or trend.

instruct [instrʌ́kt] v. (정보를) 알려 주다; 지시하다; 가르치다 (instruction n. 설명)
Instructions are clear and detailed information on how to do something.

^복^습 bottom [bάtəm] n. (아래쪽) 뒷면; 바닥; 맨 아래 (부분)
The bottom of an object is the flat surface at its lowest point.

carve [kɑːrv] v. (글씨를) 새기다; 조각하다; ~을 이뤄 내다
If you carve writing or a design on an object, you cut it into the surface of the object.

ᵇ exclaim [ikskléim] v. 소리치다, 외치다

If you exclaim, you cry out suddenly in surprise, strong emotion, or pain.

⋅ overdo [òuvərdúː] v. 지나치게 많이 쓰다; 과장하다

If you overdo an activity, you try to do more than you can physically manage.

ᵇ at once idiom 동시에; 즉시

If a number of different things happen at once or all at once, they all happen at the same time.

∶ embarrass [imbǽrəs] v. 당황스럽게 하다, 어색하게 하다; 곤란하게 하다
(embarrassed a. 어색한, 당황스러운)

A person who is embarrassed feels shy, ashamed, or guilty about something.

at one time or another idiom 한 번쯤은

At one time or another means not very often, but occasionally.

∶ count [kaunt] v. (수를) 세다; 간주하다; 중요하다; n. 셈, 계산; 수치; 사항

When you count, you say all the numbers one after another up to a particular number.

⋅ fame [feim] n. 명성

If you achieve fame, you become very well-known.

∶ fancy [fǽnsi] a. 고등 기술의; 고급의; 장식이 많은, 색깔이 화려한; v. 생각하다, 상상하다

If you describe something as fancy, you mean that it is complicated or difficult.

be left over idiom (~을 쓰고 난 뒤) 남다

If food or money is left over, it remains when the rest has been eaten or used up.

∶ treat [triːt] n. (대접하는) 특별한 것; 기쁨; v. (특정한 태도로) 대하다; 치료하다; 대접하다

If you give someone a treat, you buy or arrange something special for them which they will enjoy.

⁑hesitate [hézətèit] v. 망설이다, 주저하다; 거리끼다
If you hesitate, you do not speak or act for a short time, usually because you are uncertain, embarrassed, or worried about what you are going to say or do.

복습nod [nad] v. (고개를) 끄덕이다, 까딱하다; n. (고개를) 끄덕임
If you nod, you move your head downward and upward to show that you are answering 'yes' to a question, or to show agreement, understanding, or approval.

복습bunch [bʌntʃ] n. 다발, 묶음; (양·수가) 많음
A bunch is a group of like items or individuals gathered or placed together.

복습mighty [máiti] a. 강력한, 힘센; ad. 대단히, 굉장히
Mighty is used to describe something that is very large or powerful.

flop [flap] v. 털썩 주저앉다; ~을 떨어뜨리다; n. 실패작
If you flop into a chair, for example, you sit down suddenly and heavily because you are so tired.

prickle [prikl] v. (머리털이) 곤두서다; 까칠거리다; n. (작은) 가시; (몸이) 오싹해짐
If your skin prickles, it feels as if a lot of small sharp points are being stuck into it, either because of something touching it or because you feel a strong emotion.

⁎shove [ʃʌv] n. 힘껏 떠밂; v. (거칠게) 밀치다; 아무렇게나 놓다
A shove is a strong push.

budge [bʌdʒ] v. 약간 움직이다, 꼼짝하다; 의견을 바꾸다
If you cannot budge someone or something, you cannot make them move.

⁑regular [régjulər] a. 보통의, 평범한; 규칙적인, 정기적인
Regular is used to mean 'normal.'

⁎glance [glæns] v. 흘깃 보다; 대충 훑어보다; n. 흘깃 봄
If you glance at something or someone, you look at them very quickly and then look away again immediately.

⋅vanish [vǽniʃ] v. 사라지다, 없어지다; 모습을 감추다
If someone or something vanishes, they disappear suddenly or in a way that cannot be explained.

⋅scratch [skrætʃ] v. (가려운 데를) 긁다; 긁힌 자국을 내다; n. 긁힌 자국; 긁는 소리
If you scratch yourself, you rub your fingernails against your skin because it is itching.

trunk [trʌŋk] n. (코끼리의) 코; 나무의 몸통
An elephant's trunk is its very long nose that it uses to lift food and water to its mouth.

pat [pæt] v. 쓰다듬다; 가볍게 두드리다; n. 쓰다듬기, 토닥거리기
If you pat something or someone, you tap them lightly, usually with your hand held flat.

lick [lik] v. 핥다; 핥아먹다; n. 한 번 핥기, 핥아먹기
When people or animals lick something, they move their tongue across its surface.

company [kʌ́mpəni] n. 함께 있음; 회사; 단체
Company is having another person or other people with you, usually when this is pleasant or stops you feeling lonely.

⋅halfway [hǽfwéi] ad. (거리·시간상으로) 중간에
Halfway means in the middle of a period of time or of an event.

stuffy [stʌ́fi] a. 답답한; 딱딱한, 격식적인
If it is stuffy in a place, it is unpleasantly warm and there is not enough fresh air.

punish [pʌ́niʃ] v. 처벌하다, 벌주다; (형벌·형에) 처하다 (punishment n. 벌, 처벌)
To punish someone means to make them suffer in some way because they have done something wrong.

trick [trik] n. 장난, 속임수; 마술; v. 속이다, 속임수를 쓰다
A trick is an action that is intended to deceive someone.

복습 fellow [félou] n. 녀석, 친구; 동료; a. 동료의
A fellow is a man or boy.

★ tremble [trembl] v. (가볍게) 흔들리다; (걱정·두려움으로) 떨리다; n. 떨림, 전율
If something trembles, it shakes slightly.

복습 whisper [hwíspər] v. 속삭이다, 소곤거리다; 은밀히 말하다; n. 속삭임, 소곤거리는 소리
When you whisper, you say something very quietly, using your breath rather than your throat, so that only one person can hear you.

‡ cross [krɔːs] a. 짜증난, 약간 화가 난; v. (가로질러) 건너다; n. 십자 기호
(crossly ad. 뿌루퉁하게)
Someone who is cross is rather angry or irritated.

복습 gasp [gæsp] v. 숨이 턱 막히다, 헉 하고 숨을 쉬다; 숨을 제대로 못 쉬다; n. 헉 하는 소리를 냄
When you gasp, you take a short quick breath through your mouth, especially when you are surprised, shocked, or in pain.

★ faint [feint] v. 실신하다, 기절하다; n. 실신, 기절
If you faint, you lose consciousness for a short time, especially because you are hungry, or because of pain, heat, or shock.

★ sake [seik] n. (~을) 위함 (for the sake of idiom ~때문에)
When you do something for the sake of someone, you do it in order to help them or make them happy.

★ selfish [sélfiʃ] a. 이기적인
If you say that someone is selfish, you mean that he or she cares only about himself or herself, and not about other people.

복습 rub [rʌb] v. (손·손수건 등을 대고) 문지르다; (두 손 등을) 맞비비다; n. 문지르기, 비비기
If you rub a part of your body, you move your hand or fingers backward and forward over it while pressing firmly.

복습 honor [ánər] v. 존경하다; 수여하다; n. 영광(스러운 것); 존경, 공경
If someone is honored, they are given public praise or an award for something they have done.

smoky [smóuki] a. 연기 모양의; 연기가 많이 나는
You can use smoky to describe something that looks like smoke, for example because it is slightly blue or gray or because it is not clear.

edge [edʒ] n. 끝, 가장자리; 우위; v. 조금씩 움직이다; 테두리를 두르다
The edge of something is the place or line where it stops, or the part of it that is furthest from the middle.

swirl [swəːrl] v. 소용돌이치다, 빙빙 돌다; n. 소용돌이
If you swirl something liquid or flowing, or if it swirls, it moves round and round quickly.

brief [briːf] a. (시간이) 짧은; 간단한; v. ~에게 보고하다 (briefly ad. 잠시)
Something that happens or is done briefly happens or is done for a very short period of time.

pour [pɔːr] v. 마구 쏟아지다; 붓다, 따르다
When a liquid or other substance pours somewhere, for example through a hole, it flows quickly and in large quantities.

spout [spaut] n. (주전자 등의) 주둥이; (액체의) 분출; v. (액체를) 내뿜다
A spout is a long, hollow part of a container through which liquids can be poured out easily.

puff [pʌf] n. (공기·연기 등의) 작은 양; 훅 부는 소리;
v. (많은 양의 연기·김을) 내뿜다; 부풀어오르다
A puff is a small amount of smoke, air, or something that can rise into the air in a small cloud.

gather [gǽðər] v. (사람들이) 모이다; (여기저기 있는 것을) 모으다
If people gather somewhere or if someone gathers people somewhere, they come together in a group.

bless [bles] v. (신의) 축복을 빌다 (bless you idiom 축복이 있기를)
Bless is used in expressions such as 'God bless' or 'bless you' to express affection, thanks, or good wishes.

ᵇᵘ generous [dʒénərəs] a. 너그러운; 넉넉한

A generous person gives more of something, especially money, than is usual or expected.

ᵇᵘ tremendous [triméndəs] a. 엄청난; 굉장한, 대단한

You use tremendous to emphasize how strong a feeling or quality is, or how large an amount is.

· rest [rest] n. 나머지; 휴식; v. 쉬다; 놓이다, (~에) 있다

The rest is used to refer to all the parts of something or all the things in a group that remain or that you have not already mentioned.

· yawn [jɔːn] v. 하품하다; n. 하품

If you yawn, you open your mouth very wide and breathe in more air than usual, often when you are tired or when you are not interested in something.

· murmur [mə́ːrmər] v. 속삭이다, 소곤거리다, 중얼거리다; n. 속삭임, 소곤거림

If you murmur something, you say it very quietly, so that not many people can hear what you are saying.

프롤로그

아주 먼 옛날에, 오늘날과 같은 사람들이 살기 훨씬 전에, 모두 영원히 살고, 중요한 사람은 대부분 다정한 요정(genie)인 마법 왕국이 있었습니다. 몇몇 사악한 요정은 동굴 속에 있거나 강 밑바닥에 있어 눈에 띄지 않았습니다. 그들은 많은 탑과 안뜰 그리고 반사되는 연못이 있는 정원이 있는 성에서 통치하는, 위대한 요정 왕을 도발할 생각은 꿈도 꾸지 않았습니다.

요정 왕은 왕국의 활기찬 요정 왕자들에 대한 그의 인내심으로 유명했지만, 요정 왕비는 그가 그들을 지나치게 참아주고 있다고 생각했습니다. 그녀는 어느 날 아침 왕이 보고서와 새로운 마법 주문에 대한 제안들을 살피는 공식 알현실에서 그렇게 말했습니다.

"규율, 그게 바로 왕자들이 필요로 하는 거예요!" 그녀가 공식 알현실 벽에 걸린 마법 거울을 바로 했습니다. "세상에 맙소사! 소원을 들어주는 일, 그들이 언젠가는 하게 될 그 일은, 심각한 임무라고요."

"진정해요! 당신은 남자아이들에게 너무 엄하게 굴고 있어요." 왕이 말했고, 그러더니 그는 얼굴을 찌푸렸습니다. "하지만, 이 보고서에 쓰여있기를 그들 가운데 한 명이 정말로 몹시 나쁜

태도를 보인다고 하는군요."

"하라즈(Haraz)이지요, 그렇죠?" 왕비가 말했습니다. "그는 정말로 잘난 척하는 녀석이라고요!"

요정 왕은 하라즈 왕자를 불러들이려고 생각을 하나 보냈는데, 이는 모든 지도자가 자신이 누군가를 원할 때 해야만 하는 일이었고, 잠시 후에 어린 요정이 공식 알현실로 날아들면서, 연속 3회전을 했고, 왕좌 앞 허공에서 머물렀습니다.

"무슨 일이세요?" 그가 빙그레 웃으면서, 물었습니다.

"네가 문제야!" 왕비가 말했습니다. "여기로 내려와!"

"알겠어요." 하라즈가 말하면서, 내려왔습니다.

"네가 정말 많은 마법 장난을 치고 다니는 것 같구나." 왕이 그의 앞에 있는 보고서를 툭툭 두드리면서, 말했습니다. "몹시 짜증이 나게 하는 장난들 말이야, 이를테면 군대에서 쓰는 카펫이 계속 원만 그리며 날게 해서, 내 모든 군사들을 어지럽게 하는 일 같은 것들 말이야."

"그건 좋은 장난이었죠!" 하라즈가 웃었습니다.

"그리고 대마법사가 중요한 주문을 걸고 있는 동안에, 그의 지팡이를 소시지로 변하게 하는 일? 네가 정말 그런

짓을 했느냐?"

"하, 하! 아버지는 그의 얼굴을 봤어야만 했어요!"

"그만 웃거라!" 왕비가 소리쳤습니다. "이는 부끄러운 행동이야! 너는 심한 벌을 받아야만 해!"

"그는 단지 아이일 뿐이에요, 여보, 고작 이백 살밖에 되지 않았잖소." 왕이 말했습니다. "하지만 나는—"

"그가 어떤 짓을 더 했는지 그 누가 알겠어요?" 왕비가 마법 거울을 향해 돌아섰습니다. "거울아, 하라즈가 쳤던 바보 같은 장난이 또 뭐가 있니?"

마법 거울은 그녀의 얼굴 전체와 그녀의 드레스 앞에 사과 주스를 내뿜었습니다.

"오오오오!" 왕비가 휙 돌아섰습니다. "세상에 이럴 수가! 난 누가 저런 짓에 대한 책임이 있는지 알고 있어!"

하라즈 왕자는 미안한 듯한 표정을 지으려고 했지만, 이미 너무 늦었습니다.

"더는 못 참겠구나!" 요정 왕이 말했습니다. "너에게 램프 임무를 내리겠노라, 이 악동 녀석 같으니! 천 년 동안 램프에 대한 봉사를 해라!" 그가 왕비를 향해 돌아섰습니다. "이러면 어떻소, 여보?"

"이천 년으로 해요." 왕비가 자신의 얼굴을 닦으면서, 말했습니다.

1장 하라즈 왕자

큰 게시판이 밤중에 몸 위로 떨어져서 스탠리 램찹(Stanley Lambchop)이 납작해졌던 일을 겪은 지 거의 일 년이 다 되어가고 있었습니다. 모든 램찹 가족에게 있어서 즐겁고, 평화로운 시간이었는데, 이 특별한 저녁도 마찬가지였죠.

저녁 식사는 모두 마쳤습니다. 거실에서, 램찹 씨(Mr. Lambchop)가 자신의 신문에서 고개를 들어 보았습니다. "이게 얼마나 좋은지 몰라요, 여보." 그가 양말을 꿰매고 있는 램찹 부인(Mrs. Lambchop)에게 말했습니다. "난 내 신문을 읽는 것과 당신과 함께 있는 것을 즐기고 있고, 우리의 아들들은 그들의 방에서 공부하고 있으니 말이에요."

"그들이 그러고 있기를 바라자고요." 램찹 부인이 말했습니다. "너무나 자주, 조지(George), 그들은 공부하지 않을 핑계거리를 찾아내요."

램찹 씨가 껄껄거리며 웃었습니다. "그들이 정말 상상력이 풍부하긴 하지요." 그가 말했습니다.

그들의 방에서, 스탠리와 그의 남동생, 아서(Arthur)는, 정말로 숙제하고 있었습니다. 그들은 잠옷을 입고, 자기 잠옷 위로, 아서는 또한 자신의 마이티 맨(Mighty Man) 티셔츠를 입고 있었는데, 이는 그가 집중하는 데 도움을 주었습니다.

그들 사이에 있는 책상 위에는 그들이 찻주전자라고 생각하는 물건이 있었는데—둥글고, 다소 납작하게 눌린 주전자로 휘어진 주둥이와 들 수 있게 위에 손잡이가 달려 있었습니다. 파도가 그 여름에 그것을 굴려 해변으로, 바로 스탠리의 발로 올려 보냈습니다; 그리고 램찹 부인이 오래된 가구와 은 식기를 아주 좋아하기 때문에, 그는 그것을 이제는 고작 일주일밖에 남지 않은, 엄마의 생일에 드릴 선물로 간직해 왔습니다.

그 주전자는 어두운 녹색으로 칠해져 있었지만, 약간 갈색을 띠는 금속 줄무늬가 보였습니다. 닦으면 그것을 반짝이게 할 수 있을까 봐, 스탠리는 자신의 잠옷 소매로 손잡이를 문질렀습니다.

펑! 까만 연기가 주둥이에서 나왔습니다.

"이크!" 아서가 말했습니다. "그건 폭발할 거야!"

"찻주전자는 폭발하지 않아." 스탠리가 다시 문질렀습니다. "난 그저—"

펑! 펑! 펑! 그것들이 이제는 빠르게 나오면서, 책상 위 공중에 생긴 작은 구름을 형성하며 모여들었습니다.

"조심해!" 아서가 소리쳤습니다. "어이쿠!"

검은 구름이 빙빙 돌면서, 그 까만 것이 갈색과 파란색이 섞인 것으로 변해갔고, 그 구름의 형태를 잃기 시작했습니다. 팔이 나타났고, 그다음에는 다리가, 그리고 머리가 나타났습니다.

"준비되었건, 되지 않았건, 내가 간다!" 분명하고 어린 목소리가 말했습니다.

이제 구름은 완전히 사라졌고, 마르고 활기차게 보이는 남자아이가 책상 위 허공에 떠 있었습니다. 그는 일종의 장식된 수건을 자기 머리에 둘렀고, 헐렁한 파란 셔츠와 별나고, 펄럭거리는 갈색 바지를 입었는데, 그 다리들 가운데 하나는 주전자의 주둥이에 걸려 있었습니다.

"세상에!" 남자아이가, 자기 다리를 흔들면서, 말했습니다. "맙소사! 내가 제대로 연기를 뿜었잖아, 그리고 무섭게 생긴 구름이긴 하지만— 저것 봐!" 풀려나면서, 그는 바닥으로 둥둥 떠 내려왔고 스탠리와 아서에게 허리를 굽히며 인사했습니다.

"누가 문질렀니?" 그가 물었습니다.

형제 가운데 누구도 말을 할 수 없었습니다.

"뭐, 누군가는 했어. 요정은 그냥 찾아오지 않아, 너도 알다시피." 그 남자아이가 다시 허리를 숙여 인사했습니다. "안녕? 나는 파우지 무스타파 아슬란 미르자 멜렉 나머드 하라즈 왕자

(Prince Fawzi Mustafa Aslan Mirza Melek Namerd Haraz)야. 나를 하라즈 왕자라고 부르도록 해."

아서가 숨을 헉 하고 들이마셨고 침대 밑으로 뛰어들었습니다.

"쟤는 왜 저러는 거야?" 지니가 물었습니다. "그리고 넌 누구고, 난 어디에 있는 거야?"

"난 스탠리 램찹이고, 이곳은 미국이야." 스탠리가 말했습니다. "침대 밑에 있는 건 아서이지."

"그다지 다정한 환영 인사는 아니네." 하라즈 왕자가 말했습니다. "특히 램프 속에 웅크린 채 있던 사람에게는 말이야." 그가 자신의 뒷목을 주물렀습니다. "세상에나! 천년 동안 내 무릎을 내 턱에 바짝 붙이고 있었다고. 이번에 내가 처음 나와 본 거야."

"내가 미쳐가고 있는 게 분명해." 아서가 침대 밑에서 말했습니다. "나는 의사 선생님이 올 때까지 그냥 여기에 누워 있을 거야."

"사실은, 하라즈 왕자, 넌 여기에 실수로 왔어." 스탠리가 말했습니다. "난 저 주전자가 램프인 줄도 몰랐어. 문지른 거 때문이야? 내 말은, 그 연기가 너로 변한 거라고?"

"너 겁먹었니?" 지니가 웃었습니다. "내 생각에는, 그냥 약간의 연기가 난 다음, 내가 주둥이 위로 슉 하고 나온 거지."

"나를 놀라게 한 것은 공정하지 않아." 아서가 침대 밑에 머무른 상태에서, 말했습니다. "난 단순히 스탠리가 내 형이라서 이 방에서 살고 있을 뿐이야. 그건 형의 램프이고, 그걸 문지른 사람도 바로 형이야."

"그렇다면 내가 소원을 들어줄 사람도 그가 되겠구나." 하라즈 왕자가 말했습니다. "너에게는 안됐구나."

"난 신경 쓰지 않아." 아서가 그렇게 말했지만, 사실 신경이 쓰였습니다.

"내가 무엇이든 빌 수 있어?" 스탠리가 물었습니다. "아무거나?"

"그것이 잔인하거나 사악하거나, 또는 정말 고약한 일만 아니라면." 하라즈 왕자가 말했습니다. "나는 램프의 요정이야, 너도 알겠지만, 그리고 우리는 착한 요정이지. 그런 큰 병의 요정과는 달라. 그들은 아주 골칫거리라고."

"무언가를 빌어 봐, 스탠리 형." 아서가 미심쩍어하는 목소리로 말했습니다. "그를 시험해보라고."

"나 금방 다시 올게." 스탠리가 말했고, 거실로 갔습니다.

"있잖아요(Hey)!" 그가 램찹 부부에게 말했습니다. "맞춰 보세요?"

"건초(Hay)는 말을 위한 거란다, 스탠리, 사람을 위한 게 아니야." 램찹 씨가 자신의 신문 너머에서 말했습니다. "그걸 기억하도록 하렴."

"죄송해요." 스탠리가 말했습니다. "하지만 엄마 아빠는 절대로 맞추지 못할―"

"내 생각에는 너와 아서가 아직 너희 숙제를 끝내지 못한 것 같구나." 램챠 부인이 자신이 수선하던 것에서 고개를 들며, 말했습니다.

"우리는 숙제하고 있어요." 스탠리가 매우 빠르게 말을 하면서, 말했습니다. "하지만 저한테 램프인 것으로 밝혀진 찻주전자가 있었는데요, 제가 그것을 문질렀을 때, 연기가 나더니, 요정이 나타났어요. 그리고 그가 말하기를 제가 아무거나 소원을 빌 수 있어요. 단지 엄마 아빠에게 먼저 물어봐야 할 것 같았어요. 아서는 겁을 먹었어요, 그래서 그는 침대 밑에 숨어 있어요."

램챠 씨가 껄껄 웃었습니다. "네가 공부하는 것이 끝난 후에 그러렴, 애야." 그가 말했습니다. "하지만 금과 다이아몬드로 가득 찬 보물 상자는 절대로 안돼. 우리가 내야 할 세금을 생각해!"

"여기 너를 위한 답이 나왔구나, 스탠리." 램챠 부인이 말했습니다. "자 이제 다시 공부하렴."

"그럼, 알겠어요." 스탠리가 나가면서, 말했습니다.

램챠 부인이 웃었습니다. "세상에, 보물 상자라니! 세금은 물론이고요! 조지,

당신 정말 재미있네요."

자신의 신문 뒤에서, 램챠 씨가 다시 미소 지었습니다. "고마워요, 여보." 그가 말했습니다.

2장 무엇이든 물어보세요 바구니

"내가 부모님께 말했지만, 그들은 내 말을 믿지 않았어." 스탠리가 다시 방으로 돌아와서, 말했습니다.

"당연히 부모님이 믿지 않지." 아서는 여전히 침대 밑에 있었습니다. "찻주전자에서 사람이 펑 하고 나왔다는 것을 누가 믿겠어?"

"그건 찻주전자가 아니야." 하라즈 왕자가 말했습니다. "자 이제 그만 나오렴. 내가 연기를 낸 거에 대해서 사과할게."

아서가 침대 밑에서 기어 나왔습니다. "더는 무서운 짓을 하지 않을 거지?"

"약속할게." 요정이 말했고, 그들은 악수했습니다.

아서는 이제 기다릴 수가 없었습니다. "스탠리 형! 소원을 말해 봐!"

"우리는 그럴 수 없어." 스탠리가 말했습니다. "우리의 숙제를 다 할 때까지는 말이야."

"숙제가 뭐야?" 하라즈 왕자가 물었습니다.

형제는 깜짝 놀라서, 그를 빤히 쳐다

보다가, 스탠리가 설명했습니다. 요정은 자신의 고개를 저었습니다.

"학교가 *끝난 뒤에*, 너희가 즐겁게 놀 수 있을 때 말이야?" 그가 말했습니다. "내가 온 곳에서는, 우리는 그냥 무엇이든 물어보세요 바구니(Askit Basket)가 일을 하게 둔다고."

"글쎄, 그것들이 무엇이든 간에, 나도 하나가 있으면 좋겠어." 스탠리가 소원을 빌면 안 된다는 것을 잊고, 말했습니다.

하라즈 왕자가 웃었습니다. "오? 네 뒤를 봐."

돌아서자, 스탠리와 아서는 비치 볼 크기를 하고 붉은색과 초록색의 지그재그 줄무늬로 장식된, 큰 밀집 바구니가 책상 위 허공에 떠 있는 것을 보았습니다.

"이크!" 아서가 말했습니다. "또 무서운 것이잖아!"

"바보같이 굴지 마." 지니가 말했습니다. "그건 완벽하게 평범한 무엇이든 물어 보세요 바구니라고. 네가 알고 싶은 것이 무엇이든지 간에, 스탠리, 그냥 물어봐."

조금 바보 같다는 기분이 느끼며, 스탠리는 몸을 기울였고 바구니에 말을 했습니다. "난, 어 . . . 그게 . . . 어 . . . 내 수학 숙제에 대한 답을 얻을 수 있을까? 그건 내 책 20페이지에 있는 문제

들이야."

바구니가 규칙적인 <u>흐으으으으음</u> 하는 소리를 내었고, 그러더니 마치 TV 아나운서의 목소리처럼 깊고 풍부한 어떤 남자의 목소리가 그 속에서 나왔습니다.

"무엇이든 물어보세요 바구니에 전화 주셔서 감사합니다." 그것이 말했습니다. "죄송하지만, 우리의 답변 요정이 모두 지금 통화 중입니다. 당신의 질문은 가장 먼저 전화를 받을 수 있는 직원이 답변할 것입니다. 당신이 기다리는 동안에, 작은 요정들(Genie-ettes)에 의해 선택된 노래들을 감상하시겠습니다."

스탠리는 무엇이든 물어보세요 바구니를 쳐다보았습니다. 이제 그것에서 음악이 나오고 있었는데, 그가 큰 사무용 건물의 엘리베이터 안에서 듣곤 했던 감미롭고, 멀리서 들리는 음악과 같았습니다.

하라즈 왕자가 어깨를 으쓱거렸습니다. "어쩌겠어? 그건 매우 인기 있는 서비스라고."

딸깍 하는 소리가 났고 음악이 멈췄습니다. 이제 활기 넘치는 명랑함이 가득 찬, 여자의 목소리가 바구니에서 나왔습니다. "안녕하세요! 샤이린(Shireen)이에요! 오래 기다려주셔서 감사합니다, 그리고 지금 바로 당신에게 당신의 답을 드리도록 할게요. 첫 번째 답은: 배 5

개, 사과 6개, 바나나 8개입니다. 두 번째 답은: 톰(Tom)은 4살이고, 팀(Tim)은 7살, 테드(Ted)는 11살입니다. 세 번째—"

"잠깐만요!" 스탠리가 소리쳤습니다. "전 이 모든 것을 다 기억할 수 없어요!"

"당신의 편의를 위해서 특별히 작성된, 문서 기록이, 바구니 안에 들어 있습니다, 선생님." 발랄한 목소리가 말했습니다. "무엇이든 물어보세요 바구니에 전화 주셔서 감사합니다, 그리고 정말로 좋은 하루 보내세요!"

바구니의 뚜껑을 들어 올리자, 스탠리는 그의 답이 모두 적힌 종이 한 장을 보게 되었습니다. "오, 훌륭해!" 그가 말했습니다. "고마워요. 제 동생이 이제 말할 수 있을까요?"

아서가 자신의 목소리를 가다듬었습니다. "안녕하세요, 샤이린." 그가 말했습니다. "아서 램찹이에요. 영어 숙제로, 전 '제가 자라서 되고 싶은 것'에 대해서 써야만 해요."

"알겠어요, 램찹 씨." 바구니가 말했습니다. "아주 조금만 기다리세요, 필체가 맞는지 확인 중입니다—자! 다 됐어요!"

아서가 바구니를 열었고 자신의 필체로 뒤덮인 줄이 쳐진 종이 한 장을 발견했습니다. 그가 그것을 큰소리로 읽었습니다.

내가 자라서 되고 싶은 것
아서 램찹

내가 자라면, 나는 미국의 대통령이 되어서 더 이상 전쟁이 일어나지 않게 하는 법을 만들고 싶다. 그리고 우주 비행사를 만날 기회를 얻고 싶다. 그리고 나는 잔뜩 꾸미기만을 좋아하는 여자 아이들과 놀러 나가야 하지 않기를 바란다. 무엇보다도 나는 세상에서 가장 힘이 센 사람, 마치 마이티 맨처럼 되고 싶은데, 사람들을 다치게 하려는 것이 아니라, 그래서 모두 나에게 더 잘 해주었으면 하기 때문이다.

끝

아서가 미소 지었습니다. "좋아요!" 그가 말했습니다. "바로 내가 말하고 싶었던 내용이에요, 샤이린."

"좋아요." 바구니가 말했습니다. "자 이만 끊겠습니다! 멋진 하루 보내세요!"

형제는 작별인사를 했고, 하라즈 왕자는 바구니를 공중에서 낚아챘고 그것을 자신의 램프 옆 책상 위에 올려 두었습니다.

"자! 숙제가 끝났어." 그가 말했습니다. "그건 아주 평범한 종류의 소원이었어, 스탠리. 네가 항상 바라던 특별한 것 없니? 무언가 신나는 것 말이야?"

스탠리는 그 즉시 자신이 무엇을 가장 원하는지 알았습니다. 그는 언제나

동물을 좋아했습니다; 자신만의 동물원을 가진다면 얼마나 재미있을까요! 하지만 그건 너무 많은 공간을 차지하겠지, 그가 생각했습니다. 그렇다면 동물 딱 하나만, 진짜 독특한 애완동물로 말이야. 사자? 그래! 목줄을 착용한 애완 사자를 데리고 길을 돌아다니면 얼마나 즐거울까!

"나는 사자가 있으면 좋겠어!" 그가 말했습니다. "진짜 사자 말이야, 하지만 상냥한 녀석으로."

"진짜지만, 상냥한 사자라고." 요정이 말했습니다. "문제없어."

스탠리는 문득 사자가 사람들을 무섭게 할지도 모르고, 코끼리가 훨씬 더 재미있을지도 모른다는 것을 깨달았습니다.

"다시 말할래, 코끼리!" 그가 외쳤습니다. "사자 말고, 코끼리야!"

"뭐?" 하라즈 왕자가 말했습니다. "코끼—? 오, 맙소사! 네가 나에게 시킨 짓을 좀 봐!"

방 맞은편 허공에서 가장 독특한 머리가 생겨났는데, 코는 코끼리의 코에, 작고 앙증맞은 사자 같은 귀를 지닌 머리였습니다. 머리 뒤편으로는 사자의 갈기가 있었지만, 코끼리의 몸통과 다리는 연한 갈색을 띤 금색의 사자 털 색이었고, 마지막으로 작은 회색의 코끼리 꼬리 끝부분에 아름다운 금빛 털이 달렸습니다. 모두 다 합치자, 이 부위들은 중간 크기의 사자나 작은 코끼리 정도 크기의 동물이 되었습니다.

"와!" 스탠리가 말했습니다. "저게 뭐야?"

"사자코끼리(Liophant)야." 하라즈 왕자는 짜증이 난 것처럼 보였습니다. "그건 네 탓이야, 내 잘못이 아니라고. 네가 네 소원을 겹쳐서 말했잖아."

사자코끼리는 자기 입을 크게 열어, 반은 포효, 반은 힝힝거리는 소리인 으르러엉—끼룩! 하는 소리를 내어 그들 모두를 펄쩍 뛰게 하더니, 자신의 뒷다리로 앉아서 강아지처럼 헐떡—헐떡거렸고, 꽤 괜찮아 보였습니다.

"뭐, 우리는 상냥하다는 부분은 제대로 했네." 요정이 말했습니다. "어린 동물은 대부분 그렇지."

스탠리가 그를 쓰다듬었고, 아서는 앙증맞고 작은 귀 뒤편을 간질였습니다. 사자코끼리는 그들의 손을 핥았고 스탠리는 자신이 소원을 뒤섞은 것이 전혀 후회되지 않았습니다.

바로 그때, 침실 문에서 문을 두드리는 소리가 들렸고, 램찹 부인의 목소리가 크게 외쳤습니다. "숙제 끝났니?"

"들어오세요." 스탠리가 아무 생각 없이, 말했고, 문이 열렸습니다.

"너희 어쩜 이렇게 조용하니—" 램찹 부인이 말하기 시작하다가, 말을 멈췄습니다. 그녀의 두 눈이 천천히 방을 훑으며 하라즈 왕자에서 무엇이든 물어보세요 바구니로, 그리고 사자코끼리로 옮겨갔습니다.

"어머나!" 그녀가 말했습니다.

하라즈 왕자가 작게 허리를 굽혀 인사했습니다. "안녕하세요? 당신이 이 멋진 녀석들의 어머니인가요, 그렇죠?"

"맞아, 고마워." 램찹 부인이 말했습니다. "우리 만난 적이 있었니? 나는 기억하지 못하—"

"여기는 하라즈 왕자예요." 스탠리가 말했습니다. "그리고 저건 사자코끼리이고, 저건 무엇이든 물어보세요 바구니예요."

"맞춰 봐요." 아서가 말했습니다. "하라즈 왕자는 요정이에요, 그리고 스탠리 형은 자신이 원하는 게 무엇이든지 소원을 빌 수 있어요."

"정말 너그럽구나!" 램찹 부인이 말했습니다. "하지만 나는 잘 모르겠 . . ." 돌아서며, 그녀가 거실을 향해 외쳤습니다. "조지, 여기로 와 봐요! 매우 예상치 못한 일이 일어났어요."

"잠깐만요." 램찹 씨가 외쳤습니다. "난 내 신문에 나온 특이한 이야기를 읽는 중이에요, TV를 보는 오리에 대해서예요."

"이건 그것보다 훨씬 더 특이해요." 그녀가 말했고, 램찹 씨가 즉시 왔습니다.

"아, 그러네요." 그가 말하면서, 방을 둘러보았습니다. "그래, 나도 알겠어요. 누가 설명 좀 해보겠니?"

"제가 그 전에 하려고 했잖아요." 스탠리가 말했습니다. "기억하세요? 그거에 대한—"

"잠시만, 애야." 램찹 부인이 말했습니다.

사자코끼리가 코를 킁킁거리면서, 배고픈 듯한 소리를 냈기 때문에, 그녀는 부엌으로 갔다가 따뜻한 우유와 섞은 햄버거로 가득 찬 커다란 통을 가지고 돌아왔습니다. 사자코끼리가 먹는 동안, 스탠리는 램찹 부인에게 무슨 일이 일어났는지 말했습니다.

램찹 씨가 잠시 생각했습니다. "정말 특이하긴 하구나." 그가 말했습니다. "그리고 너에게는 얼마나 좋은 기회니, 스탠리. 하지만 나는 너희 숙제를 하는 데 무엇이든 물어보세요 바구니를 사용하는 것을 허락하지 못하겠구나, 애들아. 너희 선생님들도 마찬가지일 거야, 유감스럽지만."

"제 계획은, 그들에게 말하지 말자는 거예요." 아서가 말했습니다.

램찹 씨가 그를 오래 바라보았습니다. "넌 네가 하지 않은 일에 대해서 점수를 받고 싶은 거니?"

아서가 얼굴을 붉혔습니다. "오! 뭐, 그러면 안 될 것 같네요. . .전 아무 생각이 없었어요. 이 모든 흥분되는 일 때문에요. 아시겠죠?"

램찹 씨는 판지 조각 위에 **사용 금지**라고 적었고 그것을 무엇이든 물어보세요 바구니에 테이프로 붙였습니다.

"오늘 밤에 소원을 더 빌기에는 너무 늦었단다." 램찹 부인이 말했습니다. "하라즈 왕자, 벽장에 접이식 침대가 있어, 그러니 너는 여기서 편안하게 지낼 수 있을 거야. 내일은 토요일인데, 우리는 항상 공원에서 함께 시간을 보낸단다. 너도 우리와 함께 갈래, 응?"

"정말 고맙습니다." 요정이 말했고, 그는 스탠리와 아서가 접이식 침대를 설치하는 것을 도왔습니다.

사자코끼리는 이미 잠들어 있었고, 램찹 부인은 그의 그릇을 집었습니다. "어머나! 3파운드나 되는 좋은 햄버거였는데, 그가 전부 다 먹어 버렸어." 그녀가 불을 껐습니다. "너희 모두 잘 자렴."

침실은 상당히 어두웠지만, 약간의 달빛이 창문 사이로 비추었습니다. 자신들의 침대에서, 스탠리와 아서는 하라즈 왕자가 여전히 그의 접이식 침대 위에서 앉아 있는 것을 볼 수 있었습니다. 사자코끼리가 조용히 코를 고는 소리만 제외하고 모두 잠시 침묵을 지켰고, 요정이 말했습니다. "코 고는 소리는 미안해. 저런 코를 갖고 있어서 그럴 거야, 아마."

"괜찮아." 아서가 졸려 하면서 말했습니다. "요정도 코를 골아?"

"우리는 잠을 자지도 않아." 하라즈 왕자가 말했습니다. "너희 어머니는 정말 친절하셔서, 나는 그녀에게 그렇다고 말하고 싶지 않았어. 그녀가 기분이 상할 수도 있잖아."

"내가 깨어있도록 노력해볼게, 네가 이야기하고 싶다면." 스탠리가 말했습니다.

"괜찮아." 요정이 말했습니다. "나는 괜찮을 거야. 램프 안에서 혼자 그 모든 세월 동안 있던 후에, 누군가가 곁에 있다는 것만으로도 행복해."

3장 공원에서 일어난 일

모두 늦잠을 잤고 풍성한 아침 식사를 즐겼는데, 특히나 사자코끼리는, 2파운드나 되는 햄버거를 더 먹고, 바나나 다섯 개, 세 덩이의 빵을 먹었습니다.

그리고, 모든 램찹 가족이 테니스를 치는 것을 즐겼기 때문에, 그들은 근처에 있는 큰 공원에 있는 코트로 자신들의 라켓을 챙겨 출발했습니다. 자신의 요정 복장이 사람들을 혼란스럽게 할 것임을 깨닫고, 하라즈 왕자는 스탠리한테 바지와 셔츠를 빌렸고, 함께 갔습니다.

길에서, 그들은 램찹 씨의 오랜 대학 친구인 랠프 존스(Ralph Jones)를 만났는데, 그들이 꽤 오랫동안 보지 못했던 사람이었습니다.

"이렇게 만나서 반가워, 조지, 그리고 당신도요, 램찹 부인." 존스 씨가 말했습니다. "안녕, 아서. 안녕, 스탠리. 네가 납작했던 아이였었지? 훌륭한 모습으로 둥글게 되었구나, 내가 보기엔."

"너는 항상 좋은 기억력을 갖고 있었지, 랠프." 램찹 씨가 말했습니다. "우리 집에서 묵는 손님을 소개해줄게, 하라즈 왕자야. 그는 외국 학생인데, 우리의 생활양식을 배우기 위해 이곳에 왔지."

"안녕하세요?" 요정이 말했습니다. "전 파우지 무스타파 아슬란 미르자 멜렉 나머드 하라즈라고 해요."

"안녕?" 존스 씨가 말했습니다. "흠, 나는 가야만 할 것 같네. 안녕, 램찹 가족. 만나서 반갑구나, 파우지 무스타파 아슬란 미르자 멜렉 나머드 하라즈 왕자."

"그는 정말로 훌륭한 기억력을 갖고 있네요." 존스 씨가 떠나자 램찹 부인이 말했습니다.

그들은 다시 공원으로 향했습니다.

"하라즈 왕자가 요정이라는 걸 존스 씨가 알게 된다면 얼마나 놀랄까요?" 램찹 부인이 말했습니다. "온 세상이 깜짝 놀랄 거예요. 어머나! 우리 모두 유명해질 거예요, 확신하건대."

"전 한때 유명했어요, 제가 납작했을 때요." 스탠리가 말했습니다. "좀 지나니까 전 그걸 좋아하지 않았어요."

"나도 기억한단다." 램찹 부인이 말했습니다. "그렇다고 해도, 난 유명해진다는 것이 어떤 기분인지 직접 느껴봤으면 좋겠구나."

하라즈 왕자가 물어보는 듯이 스탠리를 보았고, 스탠리는 작게 고개를 끄덕였습니다. 요정은 미소 지었고 고개를 끄덕여 답했습니다.

그들은 도시의 가장 중요한 건물 가운데 하나인 유명한 미술관(Famous Museum of Art)을 막 지나고 있었습니다. 외국에서 온 방문객으로 가득 찬, 관광버스가 미술관 앞에서 멈췄고, 가이드가 확성기로 승객들에게 강연하고 있었습니다.

"저 나무들이 있는 곳 뒤로, 우리의 큰 도시 공원이 있습니다!" 그가 방송으로 알렸습니다. "여기, 오른쪽에는, 훌륭한 그림과 조각들로 가득 찬, 유명한 미술관이 있고— 오, 이렇게 놀라운 일이! 우리가 오늘 운이 좋네요, 여러분! 저 사람은 조지 램찹 부인이잖아요, 우리를 향해서 오고 있어요! 해리엇 램찹(Harriet Lambchop) 본인이, 직접 말이에요! 바로 저기, 테니스 라켓을 들고 있어요!"

관광객들은 즐거운 탄성을 외치면서, 자신의 자리에서 돌아서며 가이드가 가리키는 곳을 쳐다보려고 했습니다.

"무슨—? 그는 당신을 말하는 거예요, 해리엇!" 램찹 씨가 말했습니다.

"저도 그런 것 같네요." 램찹 부인이 말했습니다. "오, 맙소사! 그들이 오고 있어요!"

관광객들이 버스에서 급히 달려왔습니다. 일본인 가족이 램찹 부인에게 가장 먼저 도착했고, 모두 카메라를 들고 있었습니다.

"제발이요, 램찹 부인." 남편이 말하며, 정중하게 허리를 굽혀 인사했습니다. "사진을 찍을 영광을 주세요, 네?"

"물론이지요." 램찹 부인이 말했습니다. "전 여러분이 우리나라를 즐기기를 바라거든요. 하지만 왜 제 사진을 원하는 거지요? 저는 아닌데—"

"아니, 아니에요! 유명하고, 유명하잖아요! 유명한 램찹 부인!" 일본인 가족이 외치면서, 그들이 할 수 있는 한 빠르게 사진을 찍었습니다.

램찹 부인이 갑자기 자신의 소원이 이루어졌다는 것을 이해했습니다. "고맙구나, 하라즈 왕자!" 그녀가 말했습니다. "정말 재미있구나!"

그녀는 모든 관광객을 위해 우아하게 자세를 취했고 다수의 사인을 했습니다. 공원에서 사람들이 다시 그녀를 알아봤고, 그녀는 더 많이 자세를 취하고, 더 많은 사인을 해야 했습니다.

이제 아침나절이었고, 공원의 모든 테니스 코트는 이미 차 있었지만, 사람들이 한 코트 옆에 모인 것을 보고 그게 바로 세계 정상급의 테니스 선수인 톰 맥루드(Tom McRude)가 막 교습과 그의 스트로크를 보여주려고 한다는 것을 알았을 때 램찹 가족의 실망은 줄어들었습니다. 톰 맥루드는 그의 못된 성격과 나쁜 태도로 유명했지만, 그렇다고 해도 램찹 가족은 몹시 그를 보고 싶었습니다. 하라즈 왕자와 함께, 그들은 코트 가까이, 이 행사를 다루는 TV-뉴스 카메라 옆으로 비집고 들어갔습니다.

"여러분 가운데 누구도 저처럼 훌륭한 테니스 선수가 될 수는 없겠지요." 톰 맥루드가 말하고 있었습니다. "하지만 적어도 여러분은 저를 봤다는 황홀한 기분은 느낄 수 있겠지요."

사람들 속에 있는 작은 노부인이 작게 재채기를 했고, 그는 그녀를 노려보았습니다. "도대체 뭐가 문제예요, 할머니?"

노부인은 울음을 터뜨렸고, 친구들이 그녀를 딴 곳으로 이끌었습니다.

"정말 못된 사람이잖아!" 하라즈 왕자가 스탠리에게 속삭였습니다.

"난 나이 들고 재채기나 하는 사람들을 참을 수가 없어요!" 톰 맥루드가 말했습니다. "좋아요, 이제 제가 어떻게 제 멋진 포핸드(forehand)를 치는지 보여주겠습니다! 먼저—"

"잠깐 기다려요, 톰!" TV-뉴스 제작자가 불렀습니다. "우리가 방금 여기에 계신 해리엇 램찹을 발견했어요. 이런 특종이 있을 수가! 아마도 그녀가 우리 카메라에 대고 몇 마디의 말을 할지도 몰라요."

심지어 톰 맥루드도 인상 깊게 여겼습니다. "그 해리엇 램찹 말이에요? 와!"

"그 카메라들이 이쪽으로 돌려, 친구들!" 제작자가 램찹 부인에게 달려와서, 마이크를 내밀었습니다.

"당신을 만나서 아주 신나네요!" 그가 말했습니다. "모두 당신의 가치관에 대해 알고 싶어 해요. 가장 좋아하는 색은요? 외교 문제에 대해서는 어떻게 생각하나요? 잠옷을 입고 잠을 자나요 아니면 나이트가운을 입고?"

"그건 좀 다소 사적이지 않나요?" 램찹 씨가 물었습니다.

"조지, 그만 해요 . . . ." 램찹 부인이 마이크에 대고 말했습니다. "여러분의 따뜻한 환영에 모두 감사드려요." 그녀가 말했습니다. "전 단지 제 팬들이 이 기분 좋은 공원에서 이토록 근사한 하루를 보내고 있어 기쁘다고 말하고 싶네요."

사람들은 환호하고 손을 흔들었고,

램찹 부인도 손을 흔들어 답했고 손으로 키스를 보냈습니다. 그녀가 받는 관심을 시샘하며, 톰 맥루드는 자기 뒤에 있는 울타리 너머로 테니스공을 세게 쳐 날렸습니다.

이를 눈치챈, 램찹 부인이 다시 마이크에 대고 말했습니다. "그러면 이제, 이 위대한 챔피언에게 우리의 관심을 쏟아보아요!"

"그래!" 톰 맥루드가 으르렁거리듯 말했을 때 TV 카메라들이 다시 그에게로 휙 돌아섰고, 그는 말을 이었습니다. "난 자원해서 해 볼 사람이 필요해요. 그럼 난 대부분의 선수가 나와 비교하면 얼마나 끔찍한지 보여줄 수 있겠지요!"

램찹 씨는 챔피언과 함께 코트에 서면 정말 황홀할 거라고 생각했습니다. 자신의 라켓으로 신호를 보내면서, 그는 앞으로 나섰습니다.

톰 맥루드는 그에게 공 몇 개를 건넸습니다. "좋아요, 서브를 보내 봐요."

램찹 씨는 서브할 준비를 했습니다.

"그는 그의 발을 잘못 두었어요!" 톰 맥루드가 외쳤습니다. "그리고 그가 쥐는 방식도 잘못되었고요! 모든 것이 틀렸어요!"

이는 램찹 씨를 몹시 긴장하게 해서 그는 두 개의 공을 네트 너머가 아닌 그 속으로 서브해 버렸습니다.

"끔찍해! 끔찍하다고! 내가 어떻게 하는지 잘 봐요." 톰 맥루드가 말하면서, 코트 저편으로 달려갔습니다. 그곳에서 그가 공 다섯 개를, 너무 강하고 빠르게 서브 넣어서 램찹 씨는 처음 네 개를 완전히 놓쳤습니다. 다섯 번째 공은 라켓을 쳐 그의 손에서 떨어뜨렸습니다.

"하, 하!" 톰 맥루드가 웃었습니다. "이제 당신이 뛰는 것을 보죠!"

그는 코트를 가로지르며 날카로운 각도로 쌩쌩 소리를 내는 포핸드와 백핸드(backhand)를 치기 시작해, 그의 얼굴이 몹시 빨개지고 사실상 거의 모든 공을 놓치면서, 그가 이리저리 바쁘게 뛰어다니는 동안 램찹 씨를 바보처럼 보이게 했습니다.

다른 램찹 가족은 점점 화가 났고, 하라즈 왕자도 마찬가지였습니다. "이건 계속될 필요가 없어, 너도 알겠지만." 그가 스탠리에게 속삭였습니다.

바로 그때, 램찹 씨가 그들 앞에서 갑자기 멈추면서, 자기 라켓에 그의 무릎을 쾅 하고 부딪혔고 그는 챔피언의 강력한 서브를 또다시 놓쳤습니다.

"하, 하! 이게 바로 *내가* 교훈을 주는 방법이지!" 톰 맥루드가 외쳤습니다.

램찹 씨는 스탠리, 그다음에는 하라즈 왕자를 보았습니다. "좋아." 스탠리가 말했고, 요정은 작게 미소 지었습니다.

"고맙구나." 램찹 씨가 말했습니다.

코트로 돌아가서, 그는 사람들에게 외쳤습니다. "신사 숙녀 여러분, 전 다시 제 서브를 넣으려고 합니다!"

네트 반대편에서, 톰 맥루드가 사악한 웃음소리를 냈고 자신의 큰 라켓으로 공중을 휙휙 갈랐습니다.

램찹 씨는 공 하나를, 이번에는 네트 속이 아니라, 그것이 가야만 하는 곳으로 총알처럼 빠르게 서브를 넣었습니다. 톰 맥루드의 입이 쩍 하고 벌어지면서 공이 쌩 하는 소리를 내며 그의 옆을 지나갔습니다. "아웃!" 그가 소리쳤습니다. "공이 아웃되었어!"

사람들 속에서 목소리가 나왔습니다. "당신 부끄러운 줄 알아요!" . . . "그 공은 *라인 안에 들어 갔어요!*" . . . "저런 거짓말쟁이 같으니!" . . . "인, 인, 인!"

톰 맥루드는 자신의 주먹을 흔들었습니다. "난 당신이 또 그렇게 하지 못할 거라고 장담해요!"

램찹 씨는 서브를 셋을 더 넣었고, 각각의 공은 처음 것보다 훨씬 더 빨랐고, 마찬가지로 완벽한 위치에 꽂았습니다. 톰 맥루드는 그것들을 건드릴 수조차 없었는데, 마지막 공이 자신의 코로 튕겨 올라왔는데도 불구하고 말이지요.

그다음에 램찹 씨는 그와 경기를 하면서, 코트 주위를 빠르게 미끄러지듯이 움직였고 쉽게 모든 공을 받아쳤습니다. 강력한 포핸드로, 그는 톰 맥루드를 이쪽 모퉁이에서 저 모퉁이로 뛰어 다니게 했고; 드롭 슛(drop shot) 몇 번으로, 챔피언을 네트 쪽으로 유인하더니, 높이 서브를 쳐서 그를 다시 뒤로 급히 달려가게 했습니다. 아무도 그날 램찹 씨가 경기를 했던 것처럼 그렇게 훌륭한 테니스를 치진 못했습니다.

톰 맥루드는 곧 몹시 지치고 매우 화가 나서 계속할 수 없었습니다. 그는 자신의 라켓을 던졌고 그 위에서 펄쩍펄쩍 뛰었습니다.

"넌 그냥 운이 좋았을 뿐이야!" 그가 고함쳤습니다. "게다가, 나는 감기에 걸렸다고! 그리고 내내 햇빛이 내 눈에 들어왔어!" 사람들 사이를 밀치고 지나가면서, 그는 공원에서 도망쳤습니다.

단지 겸손하게 미소 짓고 친절한 태도로 자신의 라켓을 흔드는, 램찹 씨를 향해서 엄청난 환호가 나왔습니다. 그리고는 그는 다른 램찹 가족과 하라즈 왕자가 TV-뉴스 제작자와 함께 서 있는 곳으로 다가왔습니다.

"당신이 정말로 잘하는군요." 제작자가 말했습니다. "솔직히 말해서, 당신이 처음 저기에 나섰을 때 당신은 형편없어 보였어요."

"내가 몸을 푸는 데 시간이 좀 걸려요." 램찹 씨가 말했고 자신의 가족을 다른 곳으로 이끌었습니다.

공원을 떠나면서, 램찹 부인은 훨씬 더 많은 사인을 했고 유명한 사람들 (Famous Faces) 잡지에서 나온 기자가 그녀와 인터뷰를 하려고 집에서 기다리고 있었습니다.

"당신은 우리의 다음 호 표지에 실릴 예정이에요." 기자가 말했습니다. "당신의 몸무게는 얼마나 나가요? 당신의 인생에 대한 영화가 나올 건가요? 당신에게 첫 키스를 해준 사람은 누구였나요?"

"당신이 알 바 아니오!" 램찹 씨가 말했고, 기자는 떠났습니다.

그들은 텔레비전으로 저녁 뉴스를 보면서, 램찹 씨의 테니스 경기가 나오기를 기대했지만, 톰 맥루드가 배경에 있는, 램찹 부인의 모습이 나왔을 뿐이었습니다. "유명한 해리엇 램찹이 오늘 공원에 나왔습니다." 뉴스 진행자가 말했는데, 이는 "전 제 팬들이 이토록 근사한 하루를 보내고 있어 기쁩니다." 라고 말하는 램찹 부인을 근접 촬영한 영상이 나온 후였고, 그게 전부였습니다.

저녁 식사는 신문과 방송국 사람들이 램찹 부인을 찾는 전화로 여러 번 중단되었습니다. 그 전화들은 램찹 씨를 귀찮게 했지만, 사자코끼리에게는 그렇지 않았는데, 그는 돼지 갈빗살 네 덩이, 땅콩버터 한 병, 감자 샐러드 한 쿼트(quart), 그리고 자기 접시 아래에 있던 고무 깔개까지 먹어 치웠습니다.

4장 형제가 날아오르다

"난 불평하는 게 아니야." 아서가 말하면서, 불평했습니다. "하지만 그건 공평하지 않아. 누구는 사자코끼리를 받거나 유명해졌잖아. 나는 대통령이 되거나, 마이티 맨처럼 강해지고 싶지만, 내가 얻은 거라고는 심지어 우리가 더는 사용할 수 없는 무엇이든 물어보세요 바구니를 1분 동안 쓴 것밖에 없어."

저녁 식사가 끝난 뒤, 형제는 모두 잠옷을 입고서, 하라즈 왕자와 함께 그들의 침실에 있었습니다.

"그건 내 잘못이 아니야, 아서." 요정은 상처 받은 듯 보였습니다. "난 그저 명령을 따를 뿐이야. 문지르면, 내가 나타나지. 소원을 빌면, 내가 들어줘. 그게 전부야."

스탠리는 자신의 동생에게 미안한 기분이 들었습니다. "난 네가 대통령이 되어야 한다고 생각하지 않아, 아서." 그가 말했습니다. "하지만 나는 네가 세상에서 가장 힘이 센 사람이 되게 해달라고 빌 거야. 난 그것을 원해, 하라즈 왕자!"

"오, 좋았어!" 아서가 말했습니다.

그는 기다렸지만, 아무 일도 일어나지 않았습니다. "젠장! 그게 통하지 않았어!" 실망하며, 그가 자신의 오른쪽 주먹으로 왼손을 세게 때렸습니다.

"아아악!" 위아래로 펄쩍펄쩍 뛰면서, 아서가 고통을 덜려고 자신의 손을 퍼덕퍼덕 흔들었습니다.

"네가 세상에서 제일 강한 사람이 되었다면." 하라즈 왕자가 말했습니다. "넌 네가 무엇을 치는지에 대해 주의해야 할 거야."

"하지만 나는 여전히 나 자신처럼 느껴지는걸." 아서가 말했습니다. 자신의 몸을 시험해 보려고, 그는 한 손으로 큰 책상을 잡고 자기 머리 위로 쉽게 들어올렸습니다.

스탠리의 입이 크게 벌어졌고, 책상 서랍도 마찬가지로 열렸습니다.

연필, 구슬, 그리고 종이 집게들이 바닥으로 쏟아져 내렸습니다.

"이런!" 아서가 말했습니다.

"이건 말도 안 돼." 그가 정리하는 것을 도와주며, 하라즈 왕자가 말했습니다. "세상에서 제일 강한 사람이 되었는데, 침실에서 책상이나 들어 올리다니! 밖으로 나가서 모험을 해야지, 그게 바로 네가 있어야만 하는 곳이라고."

"우리는 지금은 그럴 수 없어." 아서가 말했습니다. "이제 잠잘 시간이 다 되었어."

스탠리에게 좋은 생각이 났습니다. "우리가 날 수 있다면 시간이 있을 거야! 우리 모두 어디론가 날아갈 수 있을까?"

"나는 항상 그럴 수 있긴 하지." 요정이 말했습니다. "너희 두 사람은, 소원을 빌면 돼."

"난 원해!" 스탠리가 외쳤습니다. "나는 것을 말이야! 아서와 나 둘 다!"

잠시 형제는 숨을 죽이며, 허공으로 휙 올라가기를 기대했습니다. 그러더니 아서가 자신의 팔꿈치로 작게 퍼덕거리는 행동을 했습니다.

"오, 이런!" 요정이 말했습니다. "그렇게 하는 게 아니야. 그냥 나는 것과 너희가 어디로 가고 싶은지 *생각해.*"

그건 효과가 있었습니다.

스탠리와 아서는 자신의 몸이 갑자기 바닥에서 몇 피트 떨어지는 것을 발견했고, 그들은 엎드린 상태에서 꽤 편안하게, 그리고 위아래, 앞 또는 뒤, 그들이 가기를 원하는 방법대로, 움직였습니다. 그건 마치 부드럽고, 보이지 않는 물속에서 수영하는 것 같았지만, 수영을 해야 한다는 노력이 필요하지 않을 뿐이었습니다. 형제가 행복하게 방에서 미끄러지듯이 돌아다니는 동안 하라즈 왕자는 조언했습니다: "네 발가락을 세워. . . . 조심해! . . . 좋아, 아주 좋아. . . . 그래, 난 이제 너희가 준비된 것 같아!"

그는 창문을 열었고 몸을 밖으로 내밀었습니다. "흐음. . . . 이 바람은 아마 위로 더 높이 갈수록 차가울 거야. 우리는 무언가를 더 입는 편이 좋겠어."

스탠리와 아서는 목욕용 가운을 입고 장갑을 꼈고, 요정은 빨간 파카와 드래곤-얼굴이 그려진 스키 마스크를 선택했습니다. 그러더니 그가 말했습니다. "멀리 우리 떠나자!" 그리고 형제는 그를 따라서 둥둥 떠서 창문을 지나, 밤 속으로 나갔습니다.

위로! 위로! 위로! 그들이 향해 갔고, 가끔 수평 비행을 하면서 더 속도를 내는 것을 연습했지만, 대부분 꾸준히 더 높이 올라갔습니다. 스탠리와 아서는 나란히 날아가면서, 서로에게서 자신감을 얻었고, 요정은 뒤에서 그들을 지켜보았습니다.

아름다운 밤이었습니다. 그들 위로 펼쳐진 하늘은 별들로 가득했습니다. 그들 아래에는 도시의 불빛이 별처럼 눈부시게 반짝였습니다. 형제의 하얀 목욕용 가운과 요정의 빨간 파카는 달빛을 받아 반짝였습니다.

그들은 큰 공원 위로 날아갔고, 그곳에서는 오케스트라가 공연하고 있었습니다. 음악이 그들에게까지 흘러 들어 왔습니다: 플루트(flute)와 바이올린(violin) 그리고 트럼펫(trumpet)의 맑고, 감미로운 선율; 심벌즈(cymbals)와 북의 깊고, 강한 음색이었습니다.

"오, 나 이걸 즐기고 있어!" 하라즈 왕자는 자신의 드래곤 마스크 너머로 외쳤습니다. "램프 안과는 전혀 달라!"

세 비행사는 손을 맞잡고 오케스트라가 자리 잡은 곳에서 나오는 휘황찬란한 불빛 주위를 빙글빙글 돌았습니다. 그건 마치 링크에서 음악에 맞춰 아이스 스케이팅을 하는 것 같았지만, 훨씬 더 재미있었습니다.

저 멀리서, 큰 비행기의 날개 불빛이 하늘을 가로지르며 깜빡였습니다.

"그걸 쫓아가자!" 스탠리가 외쳤습니다.

하라즈 왕자가 웃었습니다. "해 봐! 내가 따라갈게!"

씽! 씽! 그들의 옆으로 자신들의 팔을 뻗은 채, 스탠리와 아서는 하늘을 가로지르며 마치 로켓처럼 휙 지나갔고, 그들의 목욕용 가운이 배의 돛처럼 펄럭거렸습니다. 큰 비행기는 빨랐지만, 형제가 더 빨랐습니다. 따라잡으며, 그들은 그것 주위를 계속 날아다니면서, 창문을 통해서 승객들이 읽고 작은 쟁반에 있는 것을 먹는 것을 보았습니다.

아서는 만화책을 든 어린 소녀를 보았습니다. 그녀가 있는 창문으로 휙 하고 가까이 다가가서, 그는 자기 목을 쭉 빼며, 그녀의 어깨너머로 읽으려고 했습니다. 어린 소녀는 고개를 들어 그를 보았습니다. 못되게 굴면서, 그녀는 그가 만화책을 볼 수 없는 곳으로 그것을 내렸고, 메롱 하고 혀를 내밀었습니다. 아서도 그녀에게 메롱 하고 자신의 혀를 내밀었고, 그 어린 소녀가 노려보더니 자신의 창문에 커튼을 잡아당겨 쳐 버렸습니다.

비행기의 반대편에서는, 스탠리가 그들의 무릎 위에 있으면서, 그들을 계속 자지 못하게 하며, 우는 아기를 둔 매우 지쳐 보이는 젊은 커플을 보았습니다. 그 창문 옆으로 날아가서 그 아이가 자신을 볼 수 있게 하고서는, 그는 웃긴 표정을 지으면서, 그의 입술을 부풀리고 그의 코를 찡그렸습니다. 아기가 미소 지었고, 스탠리는 자신의 두 엄지손가락을 그의 양쪽 귀에 넣고 나머지 손가락을 꿈틀꿈틀 흔들었습니다. 아기가 다시 미소 지었고, 잠이 들었습니다.

스탠리는 다시 비행기 주위를 날아다녔고, 조종석을 지나, 반대편에 있는 아서와 합류했습니다.

조종석에는 두 조종사가 있었고, 한 사람이 스탠리가 날아서 지나가는 것을 보았습니다. 자신의 고개를 돌리자, 그는 이제 두 형제가 날개 끝부분 위에서 맴돌면서, 하라즈 왕자가 따라오기를 기다리는 것을 보게 되었습니다.

"내가 저 바깥에서 무엇을 봤는지 맞춰 봐, 버트(Bert)." 그가 말했습니다.

"하늘에 뜬 별이야, 톰(Tom), 그리고 우리 밑으로는 드넓은 바다가 있겠지." 다른 조종사가 대답했습니다.

"아니야." 톰이 말했습니다. "목욕용 가운을 입은 아이 두 명이야."

"하, 하! 장난치기는!" 버트가 말했지만, 그도 보려고 고개를 돌렸습니다.

단지 이제는 하라즈 왕자만이 날개 위에서 보였는데, 그의 파카를 펄럭이면서 그는 비행기 뒤편에서 그를 피해 숨은 아서와 스탠리를 찾고 있었습니다.

"그래서 넌 뭘 봤는데, 버트?" 자신의 시선을 계속 앞으로 곧게 두고서, 톰이 물었습니다. "목욕용 가운을 입은 두 명의 아이들이지, 그렇지?"

"틀렸어." 버트가 조용히 말했습니다. "나는 드래곤 얼굴을 하고, 스키 복장을 한 남자가 보여."

조종사들이 서로를 빤히 쳐다보더니, 다시 날개를 내다보았지만, 요정은 비행기 뒤편으로 형제와 함께하려고 날아가 버린 후였습니다.

"저기에 아무도 없어." 톰이 말했습니다. "이 일은 누구에게도 절대 말하지 말자, 버트. 알았지?"

"좋은 생각이야." 버트가 말했습니다. "그렇고말고."

그들은 계속 비행했고 더는 말할 거리가 없었습니다.

불이 켜져 환한, 거대한 원양 정기선이 아래에 있는 바다를 가로지르며 나아갔습니다.

"어서!" 아서가 외치면서, 자신의 뒤를 따르는 스탠리와 함께 쌩 하고 날아갔습니다. 또, 하라즈 왕자는 웃었고 그들이 가게 두었습니다.

거대한 배가 지닌 아름다움에 형제는 경이로워하면서 그들은 가까이 다가갔습니다. 그건 마치 각각의 갑판이 수천 개의 초에서 나는 빛으로 반짝이는 층을 이룬 듯한, 커다란 생일 케이크와 같았습니다.

"봐, 스탠리 형!" 아서가 외쳤습니다. "그들이 주갑판에서 파티를 열고 있어!"

그들은 신나는 일을 즐기려고 더 가까이 날아갔고 그때 그것이 파티가 아니라 도둑질이라는 것을 보았습니다.

주갑판은 북적였는데 왜냐하면 도둑들이 모든 승객을 줄 세워놓고서 그들의 돈과 보석을 빼앗고 있었기 때문이었습니다. 도둑들이 타고 도착했던 헬리콥터는 근처에, 선장 함교 아래에 서 있었습니다. 선장과 그의 동료 승무원들은 몸부림쳤지만, 그들은 이제 함교 위에 사슬로 묶여 있었습니다.

"우리가 무언가를 해야만 해, 스탠리 형!" 아서가 말했습니다.

함교로 쌩 하고 내려가면서, 그는 난간 너머로 아래에 있는 도둑들에게 소리쳤습니다. "멈춰라, 이 악당들아! 돈과 보석 그리고 물건들을 모두 돌려줘!"

그의 강한 힘을 사용해서, 아서는 배

의 승무원을 묶었던 밧줄과 사슬을 끊어 냈습니다. 그건 마치 그가 고작 종이를 찢는 듯했습니다.

깜짝 놀라서, 도둑들이 뒤로 비틀비틀 물러나며, 갑판 위에 돈과 보석을 모두 떨어트렸습니다.

"오, 이런!" 한 도둑이 고함쳤습니다. "넌 누구냐?"

그가 가장 좋아하는 만화책 영웅을 기억하며, 아서는 으스대지 않을 수 없었습니다. 그는 허공으로 10피트 날아올랐고 그곳에서 멈춰, 험악하게 보였습니다.

"난 마이티 아서다!" 그가 굵은 목소리로 외쳤습니다. "마이티 아서, 범죄와 싸우는 적이지!"

도둑들과 승객들 그리고 배의 승무원들에게서 감탄의 말이 나왔습니다. "정말 강하고, 날 수도 있어! ... 누가 마이티 아서가 올 것이라고 기대했겠어? ... 우리가 이렇게 운이 좋을 수가! ... 이 일은 TV에 나올 법해!"

이제 스탠리가 자기 목욕용 가운의 허리띠를 풀어헤친 채 하늘에서 급강하해 내려오자, 그의 가운이 망토처럼 그의 뒤로 펼쳐졌습니다. "난 마이티 스탠리다!" 그가 외쳤습니다. "무고한 사람들의 수호자이지!"

"나도 마찬가지야!" 아서가 소리 지르며, 자신도 그의 가운을 망토로 썼으면

좋았을 거라고 생각했습니다. "우리 둘 다 착한 일을 하지만, 난 정말로 힘이 센 사람이야!"

그는 갑자기 몇몇 도둑들이 헬리콥터를 타고 도망치려고 하는 것을 보았습니다. 그건 이미 뜨고 있었지만, 아서는 자신이 그것 바로 위에 올 때까지 공중을 가르며 휙 움직였고, 한 손으로 그것을 다시 갑판 위로 내리눌렀습니다. 겁먹은 도둑들이 뛰쳐나왔을 때, 배의 승무원들이 그들을 붙잡아서 묶었습니다.

이제 승객들은 훨씬 더 깜짝 놀랐습니다. 그들은 "당신 저거 봤어요?" 그리고 "마이티 아서와 마이티 스탠리, 같은 날 두 사람을 다 보다니!" 또 "이건 TV에 나오는 것보다 더 좋아요!"라고 말했습니다.

형제는 배 위에서 빙빙 돌고 있었던, 하라즈 왕자와 함께 하려고 위로 날아갔습니다. "얼마나 잘난 척하기 좋아하는 한 쌍인지!" 요정이 말했습니다. "내가 예전에 그랬던 것보다 더 심하다니까."

그들이 집을 향해 출발하자, 고마워하는 승객들과 승무원의 환호가 그들의 뒤에서 울려 퍼졌습니다. "우리를 구해준 사람들에게 만세!" 그들이 들었는데, 그리고는 "특히 마이티 아서에게!" 그리고 잠시 후에는 이런 말도 들렸지요. "물론, 마이티 스탠리도요!"

곧 큰 배는 아래에 펼쳐진 검은 바다에 있는 작은 불빛으로 된 윤곽에 지나지 않게 되었고, 마지막 환호는 단지 세차게 부는 바람결에 들리는 속삭임에 불과했습니다: "범죄와 . . . 싸우는 . . . 적 . . . 그리고 . . . 무고한 . . . 사람들의 . . . 수호자를 . . . 위해 . . . 만세 삼창!"

형제는 매우 자랑스럽게 느꼈지만, 이는 피곤한 모험이었기에, 그들은 도시가 시야에 들어왔을 때 유감스럽지 않았습니다.

5장 마지막 소원

침실로 다시 날아갔을 때, 세 모험가들은 램찹 부부가 걱정하며 기다리는 것을 발견했습니다. 방금 커다란 그릇에 담긴 초콜릿 쿠키와 우유와 섞인 스파게티를 다 먹어 치웠던, 사자코끼리는 잠들어 있었습니다.

"정말 다행이야!" 램찹 부인이 달려가 그녀의 아들들을 안아주었습니다.

"너희 어디에 있다 온 거니?" 램찹 씨는 엄했습니다. "그건 하라즈 왕자, 너니, 드래곤 얼굴 뒤에 있는 사람이?"

요정은 자신의 마스크를 벗었습니다. "걱정하셨어요? 죄송해요. 우리는 잠깐 비행하러 나갔던 거예요."

"엄마 아빠 이것 좀 들어 보세요!" 아서가 말했습니다. "엄마 아빠는 그냥 보는 것만으로는 모르시겠지만, 전 세상에서 제일 강한 사람이에요, 그리고—"

"그 가운과 장갑을 벗으렴." 램찹 부인이 말했습니다. "지나치게 더워지는 건 현명하지 않단다."

그녀가 계속 말하는 동안, 그들은 자신들의 물건을 정리했습니다. "대단한 저녁이야! 전화가 한시도 쉬지 않고 울렸단다. 난 네 개의 TV 쇼에 나오고, 새 비누를 광고해달라고 부탁받았지—그들은 욕조에 들어간 내 모습을 사진으로 찍고 싶다고 했어, 그래서 물론 나는 안 된다고 말했지!—그다음엔, 창문이 열려있고 너희 세 사람이 *사라졌잖니!* 얼마나 무섭던지!"

"우리는 우리가 금방 돌아올 거라고 생각했어요." 스탠리가 사과하며 말했다. "우리는 그렇게 많은 흥미로운 일들이 일어날 줄 몰랐어요."

모두 앉았고, 스탠리는 아서가 힘이 세지길 바란다는 소원을 빌었던 것, 그리고 날았던 것, 또 비행기를 쫓아간 것과 배 위에 있던 도둑들에 대해서 이야기했습니다. 스탠리가 이야기를 끝냈을 때 램찹 부부는 둘 다 깊은 한숨을 내쉬었습니다.

"보아하니, 하라즈 왕자." 램찹 씨가 말했습니다. "소원이 이루어졌을 때 예상치 못했던 결과가 종종 생기는 것 같구나."

"오, 그럼요." 요정이 말했습니다. "그게 바로 제가 램프 안에 들어가게 된 까닭이지요."

"단지 무엇이든 물어보세요 바구니 문제만이 아니야." 램찹 씨가 말했습니다. "램찹 부인이 유명해진지 하루도 채 되지 않았고, 벌써 그녀는 녹초가 되어 버렸고 그녀의 모든 사생활을 잃어버렸어. 그리고 비록 톰 맥루드가 그가 겪은 일을 자초하긴 했지만, 그의 테니스 실력은 자연스러운 능력에서 나온 것이지. 난 마법을 사용해서 그를 창피하게 했던 것이 자랑스럽지 않구나."

"그리고 아서의 강력한 힘은 다른 남자아이들이 그를 두려워하게 할 거야." 램찹 부인이 말했습니다. "그리고 날아다니는 것, 범죄자와 얽히는 일 말이야 . . . 맙소사! 우리는 이 모든 것을 고려해야만 해. 내가 코코아를 만들어 올게. 그건 심각하게 생각을 해야만 할 때 도움이 되거든."

모든 사람이 그녀가 부엌에서 가져온, 각각의 컵에 마시멜로(marshmallow)가 들어간, 맛있는 코코아를 즐겼습니다. 램찹 가족은 조용히 앉아서, 음료를 마시며 생각했습니다. 문제를 일으켜서 미안하다고 두 번이나 이야기했던, 하라즈 왕자는 이리저리 서성이기 시작

했습니다. 사자코끼리는 여전히 잠들어 있었습니다.

마침내 램찹 씨가 자신의 컵을 내려놓았고 헛기침을 했습니다. "자, 집중해 주세요." 그가 말했고, 그들은 모두 그를 보았습니다.

"이게 내 생각이야." 그가 말했습니다. "요정들과 그들의 마법, 하라즈 왕자는 멀고 먼 나라와 아주 오랜 옛날에는 적절했겠지만, 램찹 가족은 언제나 꽤 정상적인 사람들이었고, 이곳은 미국이고, 시대가 오늘이야. 우리는 네가 보여 준 그 흥미로운 일은 고맙게 여기지만, 이제는 내가 물어봐야 하겠구나: 스탠리가 그가 빌었던 모든 소원을 취소할 수 있니?"

"사실은, 가능해요." 요정이 말했습니다.

"당신 정말 똑똑해요, 조지!" 램찹 부인이 외쳤습니다.

아서가 한숨 쉬었습니다. "전 모르겠어요. . . . 전 날아다니는 게 정말 좋았어요. 하지만 매우 강해지는 거에 대해서는, 아무도 저와 함께 놀지 않으려고 할 것 같네요."

"전 무엇보다 사자코끼리가 걱정돼요." 스탠리가 말했습니다. "우리가 그냥 그를 기르면 안 돼요?"

"그는 무척 사랑스럽지." 램찹 부인이 말했습니다. "하지만 그는 먹는 것을 절

대로 멈추지 않아! 우리는 그를 기르는 것을 감당할 수가 없단다."

"슬프지만, 사실이지." 램찹 씨가 말했습니다. "이제 제발 우리에게 말해주렴, 하라즈 왕자, 무엇을 하면 되는지 말이야."

"그건 반대 소원이라고 불러요." 요정이 책상에서 작은 초록색 램프를 들었고 그것을 뒤집었다. "설명서가 바로 여기 바닥에 있을 거예요. 보자. . . ."

그는 램프의 밑에 새겨진 글자들을 살펴보았습니다. "아주 간단하게 보이네요. 각각의 소원은 따로따로 반대로 뒤집어야만 해요. 전 그냥 '만드로노(Mandrono)!'라고 말하고—" 그의 목소리가 커졌습니다. "오, 세상에! 이럴 수가! 거기 있는 작은 원 보여요? 이건 훈련용 램프예요! 충분한 양의 소원이 남지 않았을 수도 있어요!"

"훈련용 램프라고?" 램찹 씨가 소리쳤습니다. "그게 뭔데?"

"그것들은 저처럼 초보자를 위한 거예요, 그래서 우리가 한 사람을 위해 지나치게 힘을 쓰지 않도록 말이에요." 하라즈 왕자가 불행하다는 듯이 말했다. "원 안에 있는 작은 '15', 그게 제가 스탠리를 위해 쓰도록 허용된 모든 소원의 수예요."

램찹 가족이 모두 동시에 말했습니다. "뭐? . . . 넌 우리에게 그렇게 말한 적이 없었잖아! . . . 고작 열다섯 개라고? . . . 오, 이런!"

"제발, 전 이미 창피해요." 얼굴이 몹시 붉어진, 요정이 말했습니다. "훈련용 램프라니! 마치 내가 아기라도 되는 것처럼!"

"우리는 모두 초보자일 때가 있어, 한 번쯤은." 램찹 씨가 말했습니다. "중요한 것은, 열다섯 개의 소원이면 충분할까?"

요정은 자신의 손가락으로 수를 헤아리며 자신이 맞게 세는지 확인했습니다. "무엇이든 물어보세요 바구니, 사자 코끼리—운이 좋았어, 그를 두 개로 안 쳐도 되니까!—그거까지 두 개. 그리고 램찹 부인을 위한 유명세와 멋진 테니스 실력, 그것까지 네 개이지. 아서가 강해지게 하는 것이 다섯 개, 아서 그리고 스탠리를 날게 해주는 것까지 하면 두 개 더. . ." 그가 미소 지었습니다. "일곱 개, 그리고 반대로 뒤집는 것에 일곱 개를 쓰면 열네 개예요! 일종의 작별 선물로 하나의 소원이 남겠네요!"

"다행이구나!" 램찹 부인이 주저했습니다. "정말 시간이 몹시 늦었어. 네가 지금 소원을 뒤집는 것을 시작할 수 있겠니, 네 생각에는?"

하라즈 왕자가 고개를 끄덕였습니다. "제가 가족 전체를 한 번에 묶어서 처리할게요. 어디 보자 . . . 힘, 유명세, 테니스, 두 명이 나는 것. 준비됐니, 아서? 이 이후에는 더는 마이티 맨이 될 수 없어, 안타깝지만.”

“내가 약해졌다고 느끼게 될까?” 아서가 물었습니다. “내가 털썩 쓰러지게 될까?”

요정이 자신의 고개를 저었습니다. “만드로노!” 그가 말했습니다. “만드로노, 만드로노, 만드로노, 만드로노!”

아서는 자기 목 뒤에 난 머리털이 바짝 서는 것을 느꼈습니다. 그 오싹한 기분이 멈추었을 때, 그는 큰 책상을 밀어보았지만, 그것을 조금도 움직일 수 없었습니다.

“난 그냥 다시 평범한 나 자신이 되었네.” 그가 말했습니다. “할 수 없지.”

“그리고 난 다시 그냥 해리엇 램찹이 되었고.” 램찹 부인이 말하면서, 미소 지었습니다. “중요하지 않은 사람 말이야.”

“우리 모두한테 있어서, 여보, 당신은 우리가 아는 가장 중요한 사람이에요.” 램찹 씨가 말했습니다. “아서, 너는 어제 그랬던 것과 마찬가지로 강하단다. 그걸 그렇게 생각하렴.”

요정은 남은 자기 코코아를 마셨습니다. “내가 어디까지 했더라? 오, 맞아 . . .” 그가 무엇이든 물어보세요 바구니를 힐끗 보았습니다. “만드로노!” 바구니가 사라졌습니다. “이제 딱 사자코끼리만 있네.” 그가 말했습니다.

모든 사람이 사자코끼리를 보았는데, 그 녀석은 이제 구석에서 일어나 앉아서, 자신의 코끼리 코로 자기 사자 귀 뒤편을 긁고 있었습니다. 스탠리는 그를 쓰다듬었고, 사자코끼리는 그를 핥았습니다.

“얼마나 다정한지!” 램찹 부인이 말했습니다. “조지, 혹시 말이에요. . . ?”

“사자코끼리를 진정으로 행복하게 하는 것은.” 요정이 말했습니다. “넓은 공간, 그리고 다른 사자코끼리와 함께 있는 거예요.”

“그럼 그를 그런 곳으로 보내줘.” 스탠리가 용감하게 말하며, 다시 쓰다듬었습니다. 사자코끼리는 쓰다듬는 도중에 반쯤 사라졌습니다.

잠시 아무도 말하지 않았습니다.

“잘했어, 스탠리.” 램찹 씨가 다정하게 말했습니다. “그리고 이제 넌 마지막으로 빌 소원을 생각해야만 해.”

스탠리가 생각하는 동안, 램찹 부인은 모든 코코아 컵을 모았습니다. “넌 이제 어디로 가게 되니, 하라즈 왕자?” 그녀가 말했습니다.

“갑갑한 작은 램프 안으로 돌아가겠죠.” 요정이 말했습니다. “그러고 나서 기다리고, 기다리고, 또 기다릴 거예요! 아마도, 셀 수 없이 많은 시간을요. 그게 지나치게 많은 장난을 친 제 벌이에요. 제 친구들이 저에게 경고했었지만,

저는 듣지 않았어요."

그가 한숨 쉬었습니다. "모세프 (Mosef), 알리(Ali), 벤 시파(Ben Sifa), 어린 파우즈(Fawz). 정말 좋은 친구들이에요! 전 제가 램프 안에 혼자 있을 때 그들을 생각해요, 그들이 보내고 있을 즐거운 시간을요. 게임, 자유. . . ." 그의 목소리가 떨렸고, 램찹 가족은 그를 매우 안타깝게 여겼습니다.

문득, 아서에게 좋은 생각이 났습니다. 그는 그걸 스탠리에게 속삭였습니다.

"왜 귓속말을 하는 거야?" 요정이 퉁명스럽게 말했습니다. "그 마지막 소원을 빌도록 해, 스탠리, 그럼 나는 다시 연기가 되어 내 램프 속으로 들어갈 거야."

형제는 서로에게 미소를 지어 보였습니다. "좋은 생각이지, 그렇지?" 아서가 말했습니다.

"오, 그래!" 스탠리가 요정에게로 돌아섰습니다. "이게 내 마지막 소원이야, 하라즈 왕자. 나는 네가 램프 안에 머무는 것이 *아니라*, 네가 왔던 곳으로 돌아가서, 네 요정 친구들과 함께하며 지금부터 영원히, 그들과 즐겁게 지내기를 바라!"

하라즈 왕자가 숨을 헉 하고 들이마셨습니다. 그의 입이 쩍 벌어졌습니다.

램찹 씨는 그가 기절이라도 할까 봐 걱정했습니다. "너 괜찮니?" 그가 물었습니다. "스탠리가 너를 자유롭게 하면 안 되는 거니?"

"네, 네. . . 그건 허용되는 일이에요." 요정이 조용하게 말했습니다. "하지만 누구도 결코 요정을 위해서 소원을 빈 적이 없었어요. 지금까지는요."

"사람들이 얼마나 이기적일 수 있는지 말이야!" 램찹 부인이 말했습니다.

하라즈 왕자가 자신의 두 눈을 비볐습니다. "이 가족은 정말로 훌륭해요." 그가 말하면서, 미소 짓기 시작했습니다. "전 여러분 모두에게 감사해요. 램찹이라는 이름은 언제나, 요정들이 만나는 곳이라면 존경받을 거예요."

이제 커다란 미소를 지으며, 그는 램찹 가족과 한 사람씩 악수했습니다. 마지막 악수는 스탠리와 했고, 요정은 벌써 몸 주변이 약간 연기가 되어 있었습니다. 그가 스탠리의 손을 놓았을 무렵에는, 그는 완전히 연기가 되었고, 어두운 구름이 잠시 책상 위에 놓인 램프를 휘감더니, 주둥이를 통해 안으로 쏟아져 들어가다가 연기 한 조각도 남지 않았습니다.

완전히 놀라워하며, 램찹 가족은 램프 주위에 모였고, 잠시 후 아서가 자신의 입술을 주둥이에 대었습니다.

"잘 가, 하라즈 왕자!" 그가 외쳤습니다. "좋은 여행이 되길 바랄게!"

램프 안에서, 멀리서 들려오는 듯한 목소리가 답했습니다. "모두 행운을 빌어요. . . ." 그다음에 방에는 침묵만이 흘렀습니다.

램찹 씨가 가장 먼저 말을 했습니다. "난 네가 자랑스럽구나, 스탠리." 그가 말했습니다. "네 마지막 소원은 너그럽고 친절했어."

"사실, 그건 제 생각이었어요." 아서가 말했고, 램찹 부인이 그의 머리 위에 입을 맞췄습니다. "자 이제 침대로 가렴, 얘들아." 그녀가 말했습니다. "내일은 또 다른 하루가 될 테니까."

스탠리와 아서는 침대로 들어갔고, 그녀가 불을 껐습니다.

"램프는 깜짝 생일 선물이어야만 했어요." 스탠리가 졸린 목소리로 말했습니다. "이제는 전혀 깜짝 놀라지 않게 되었어요."

"나는 어쨌거나 그것을 좋아할 거란다." 램찹 부인이 말했습니다. "그리고 하라즈 왕자는 엄청나게 놀랄만한 일이었어. 잘 자렴, 얘들아."

그녀는 그들 모두에게 입맞추었고, 램찹 씨도 역시 입맞추고는, 그들은 나갔습니다.

형제는 잠시 어둠 속에서 조용하게 누워 있었는데, 그때 스탠리가 한숨 쉬었습니다. "난 조금 사자코끼리가 그리워." 그가 말했습니다. "하지만 난 다른 것에 대해서는 신경 쓰지 않아."

"나도 마찬가지야." 아서가 하품했습니다. "세상에, 스탠리 형, 잘 자."

"잘 자." 스탠리가 말했습니다. "맙소사."

"만드로노." 아서가 중얼거렸고 곧 그들은 둘 다 잠이 들었습니다.

끝

Prologue

1. D The few wicked genies kept out of sight in caves or at the bottoms of rivers.

2. A The Genie King was noted for his patience with the high-spirited genie princes of the kingdom, but the Genie Queen thought he was much *too* patient with them. She said so one morning in the throne room, where the King was studying reports and proposals for new magic spells. "Discipline, that's what they need!" She adjusted the Magic Mirror on the throne room wall. "Florts and collibots! Granting wishes, which they'll be doing one day, is serious work."

3. D The Genie King sent a thought to summon Prince Haraz, which is all such a ruler has to do when he wants somebody, and a moment later the young genie flew into the throne room, did a triple flip, and hovered in the air before the throne.

4. B "It seems you have been playing a great many magical jokes," said the King, tapping the reports before him. "Very *annoying* jokes, such as causing the army's carpets to fly only in circles, which made all my soldiers dizzy."

5. C The Queen turned to the Magic Mirror. "Mirror, what other dumb jokes has Haraz played?" The Magic Mirror squirted apple juice all over her face and the front of her dress. "Ooooohh!" The Queen whirled around. "Florts and collibots! I know who's responsible for that!" Prince Haraz tried to look sorry, but it was too late. "That does it!" said the Genie King. "Lamp duty for you, you rascal! One thousand years of service to a lamp."

Chapter 1

1. C On the desk between them was what they supposed to be a teapot—a round, rather squashed-down pot with a curving spout, and a knob on top for lifting. A wave had rolled it up onto the beach that summer, right to Stanley's feet; and since Mrs. Lambchop was very fond of old furniture and silverware, he had saved it as a gift for her birthday, now only a week away.

2. D The pot was painted dark green, but streaks of brownish metal showed through. To see if polishing would make it shine, Stanley rubbed the knob with his pajama sleeve.

3. B *Puff!* Black smoke came from the spout. "Yipe!" said Arthur. "It's going to explode!" "Teapots don't explode." Stanley rubbed again. "I just—" *Puff! Puff! Puff!* They came rapidly now, joining to form a small cloud in the air above the desk. "Look out!" Arthur shouted. "Double yipes!"

4. A "Can I wish for anything?" Stanley asked. "Anything at all?" "Not if it's cruel or evil, or really nasty," said Prince Haraz.

5. B "We were doing it," said Stanley, talking very fast, "but I have this pot that turned out to be a lamp, and when I rubbed it, smoke came out, and then a genie, and he says I can wish for things, only I thought I should ask you first. Arthur got scared, so he's hiding under the bed." Mr. Lambchop chuckled. "When your studying is done, my boy," he said. "But no treasure chests full of gold and diamonds, please. Think of the taxes we would pay!"

Chapter 2

1. B "We can't," Stanley said. "Not till our homework is done." "What's homework?" asked Prince Haraz. The brothers stared at him, amazed, and then Stanley explained. The genie shook his head. "After schooltime, when you could be having fun?" he said. "Where I come from, we just let Askit Baskets do the work." "Well, whatever they are, I wish I had one," said Stanley, forgetting he was not supposed to wish.

2. C Arthur smiled. "That's fine!" he said. "Just what I wanted to say, Shireen."

3. C "I wish for a lion!" he said. "Real, but friendly." "Real, but friendly," said the genie. "No problem." Stanley realized suddenly that a lion would scare people, and that an elephant would be even greater fun. "An elephant, I mean!" he shouted. "Not a lion. An elephant!" "What?" said Prince Haraz. "An eleph—? Oh, collibots! Look what you made me do!"

4. A Stanley patted him, and Arthur tickled behind the neat little ears. The

Liophant licked their hands and Stanley was not at all sorry that he had mixed up his wish.

5. D "But I do not approve of using the Askit Basket for your homework, boys. Nor will your teachers, I'm afraid." "My plan is, let's not tell them," Arthur said. Mr. Lambchop gave him a long look. "Would you take credit for work you have not done?" Arthur blushed. "Oh! Well, I guess not . . . I wasn't thinking. Because of all the excitement, you know?" Mr. Lambchop wrote NOT IN USE on a piece of cardboard and taped it to the Askit Basket.

Chapter 3

1. D "You always did have a fine memory, Ralph," Mr. Lambchop said. "Let me introduce our houseguest, Prince Haraz. He is a foreign student, here to study our ways."

2. A "I was famous once, when I was flat," Stanley said. "I didn't like it after a while." "I remember," said Mrs. Lambchop. "Nevertheless, I wish I knew myself what being famous feels like." Prince Haraz looked at Stanley in a questioning way, and Stanley gave a little nod. The genie smiled and nodded back.

3. B It was now midmorning, and all the park's tennis courts were occupied, but the Lambchops' disappointment lessened when they saw a crowd gathered by one court and learned that Tom McRude, the world's best tennis player, was about to lecture and demonstrate his strokes.

4. C Mr. Lambchop thought it would be thrilling to share a court with a champion. Signaling with his racket, he stepped forward. Tom McRude handed him some balls. "Okay, try a serve." Mr. Lambchop prepared to serve. "He's got his feet wrong!" Tom McRude shouted. "And his grip is wrong! Everything is wrong!" This made Mr. Lambchop so nervous that he served two balls into the net instead of over it. "Terrible! Terrible! Watch how I do it," said Tom McRude, running to the far side of the court.

5. B They watched the evening news on television, hoping Mr. Lambchop's tennis would be shown, but only Mrs. Lambchop appeared, with Tom McRude in the background. "The celebrated Harriet Lambchop was in the park today," said the newscaster, after which came a close-up of Mrs. Lambchop saying, "I'm glad my fans are having such a lovely day," and that was that.

Chapter 4

1. A Stanley felt sorry for his brother. "I don't think you should be President, Arthur," he said. "But I'll wish for you to be the strongest man in the world. I wish it, Prince Haraz!"

2. C "I wish!" shouted Stanley. "Flying! Arthur and me both!" For a moment the brothers held their breath, expecting to be swept up into the air. Then Arthur tried small flapping movements with his elbows. "Oh, collibots!" said the genie. "Not like that. Just *think* of flying, and where you want to go."

3. B "So what do you see, Bert?" asked Tom, keeping his own eyes straight ahead. "Two kids in bathrobes, right?" "Wrong," said Bert quietly. "I see a guy in ski clothes, with a dragon face." The pilots stared at each other, then out at the wing again, but the genie had flown to join the brothers behind the plane. "Nobody there," said Tom. "Let's never mention this to anyone, Bert. Okay?" "Good idea," said Bert. "Definitely."

4. B They flew closer to enjoy the fun and saw then that it was not a party, but a robbery. The main deck was crowded because robbers had lined up all the passengers and were taking their money and jewelry.

5. A He saw suddenly that several robbers were trying to escape in the helicopter. It was already rising, but Arthur flashed through the air until he was directly above it, and with one hand pushed it back down onto the deck. When the frightened robbers jumped out, the ship's officers grabbed them and tied them up.

Chapter 5

1. B "It seems, Prince Haraz," Mr. Lambchop said, "that there are often unexpected consequences when wishes come true." "Oh, yes," said the genie. "That's what got me into a lamp." "It's not just the Askit Basket problem," Mr. Lambchop said. "Mrs. Lambchop has been famous less than a day, and already she is exhausted and has lost all her privacy."

2. A "Dear me! We must consider all this. I will make hot chocolate. It is helpful when there is serious thinking to be done."

3. C "Here is my opinion," he said. "Genies and their magic, Prince Haraz, are fine for faraway lands and long-ago times, but the Lambchops have always been quite natural people, and this is the United States of America, and the time is today. We are grateful for the excitement you have offered, but now I must ask: Is it possible for Stanley to *un*wish all the wishes he has made?"

4. C "A training lamp?" exclaimed Mr. Lambchop. "What is that?" "They're for beginners like me, so we don't overdo for one person," Prince Haraz said unhappily. "The little 'fifteen' in the circle, that's all the wishes I'm allowed for Stanley."

5. B "Here is my last wish, Prince Haraz. I wish for you *not* to stay in the lamp, but to go back where you came from, to be with your genie friends and have good times with them, forever from now on!"

스탠리와 요술램프
(Stanley and the Magic Lamp)

1판 1쇄   2017년 9월 4일
1판 6쇄   2021년 8월 9일

지은이   Jeff Brown
기획   이수영
책임편집   김보경 정소이
콘텐츠제작및감수   롱테일북스 편집부
저작권   김보경
마케팅   김보미 정경훈

펴낸이   이수영
펴낸곳   (주)롱테일북스
출판등록   제2015-000191호
주소   04033 서울특별시 마포구 양화로 113(서교동) 3층
전자메일   helper@longtailbooks.co.kr
(학원 · 학교에서 본 도서를 교재로 사용하길 원하시는 경우 전자메일로 문의주시면
자세한 안내를 받으실 수 있습니다.)

ISBN 979-11-86701-39-3 14740

롱테일북스는 (주)북하우스 퍼블리셔스의 계열사입니다.

이 도서의 국립중앙도서관 출판예정도서목록(CIP)은 서지정보유통지원시스템(http://seoji.nl.go.kr)과
국가자료종합목록 구축시스템(http://kolis-net.nl.go.kr)에서 이용하실 수 있습니다.
(CIP 제어번호 : CIP2017020084)